MW00396856

String Stories:
A Creative,
Hands-On Approach
for Engaging Children
in Literature

Belinda Holbrook

Linworth Publishing, Inc.
Worthington, Ohio

This book is dedicated to Nate, for all his help with the pictures,
and to Dennis, for his constant support and encouragement.

I am indebted to Quan Vi for sharing his computer knowledge.

Library of Congress Cataloging-in-Publication Data

Holbrook, Belinda.
    String stories : a creative, hands-on approach for engaging children in literature /
Belinda Holbrook.
        p. cm.
    Includes bibliographical references and index.
    ISBN 1-58683-063-5 (perfectbound)
    1. Storytelling. 2. String figures. I. Title.

Z718.3 .H65 2002
027.62'51--dc21

2002032443

Published by Linworth Publishing, Inc.
480 East Wilson Bridge Road, Suite L
Worthington, Ohio 43085

Copyright © 2002 by Linworth Publishing, Inc.

All rights reserved. Purchasing this book entitles a librarian to reproduce activity sheets for use in the library within a school or entitles a teacher to reproduce activity sheets for single classroom use within a school. Other portions of the book (up to 15 pages) may be copied for staff development purposes within a single school. Standard citation information should appear on each page. The reproduction of any part of this book for an entire school or school system or for commercial use is strictly prohibited. No part of this book may be electronically reproduced, transmitted or recorded without written permission from the publisher.

ISBN 1-58683-063-5

5 4 3 2 1

Table of Contents

Credits

Thank you to the following people for giving permission to use their stories:

"The Balloon" from *A Story about String: String Stories from New Mexico's Storyfiesta™*. Originally created by Dorothy Gruber for Storytellers International's™ Storyfiesta™.

"Saving the Princess," Philip Noble.

"The Mouse Family" from *A Story about String: String Stories from New Mexico's Storyfiesta™*. Originally created by Norma J. Livo for Storytellers International's™ Storyfiesta™.

"Old Man Coyote and the Little Rabbit" from *A Story about String: String Stories from New Mexico's Storyfiesta™*. Originally created by Esther Martinez (Blue Water) for Storytellers International's™ Storyfiesta™.

"The Orange Mouse," Audrey Collinson Small, © 2002. All rights reserved.

"Alpine Cow Series," original string figures by Axel Reichert.

"Clown King: A Cat's Cradle Tale," Audrey Collinson Small, © 2002. All rights reserved.

"Mouse Face Series," as collected by Axel Reichert.

"African Bat," Valerie Baadh (after traditional tale and figure from West Africa).

"Totanguak" from *When the Lights Go Out: Twenty Scary Tales to Tell*, Margaret Read MacDonald ©____. Published by The H.W. Wilson Company.

"Anansi the Spider," from *String Things… Stories, games and fun!* Barbara G. Schutzgruber, © 1995. All rights reserved.

"The Two Old Women," David Titus.

"The Park," Crystal Brown.

"The Leprechaun," Crystal Brown.

"The Mother and the Ogre," Crystal Brown.

"Going Fishing," Brian Cox.

"Jack and the Beanstalk: David Novak's Rhyme and String Version," David Novak, story and original string figures, © 1993.

Introduction

Background

Many people are acquainted with the childhood game of Cat's Cradle, which begins with the weaving of a loop of string around two fingers on the hands of one player. Another player then removes the loop in such a way that it ends up in a different pattern on his or her hands. The game continues indefinitely as the players take turns removing the loop. Cat's Cradle is probably the most well known of all string figures, so well known that some people call all string figures Cat's Cradles. Most string figures, however, are an individual effort and often represent common objects, animals, or things in nature. String figures have been part of the cultures of many native people from around the world for hundreds, maybe even thousands, of years.

Purpose of the Book

This book is a collection of stories that uses string figures to tell the stories. Some are traditional stories that have evolved over the years, some are adapted from old tales to become more interesting to current listeners, and some use traditional string figures to tell new, contemporary stories. Some stories also include new string figures. Each story is accompanied by step-by-step illustrated instructions for creating the string figures. Librarians, teachers, and storytellers will find it to be a unique collection. String figure enthusiasts will also be interested. While stories told with string figures have appeared in publications before, this is the first book that is dedicated solely to string figure stories.

Content of the Book

Chapter I begins with a brief history of string figures, followed by a section teaching the basics to those who have never tried string figures. String figure notation is explained in detail. Of course, the stories themselves are the main focus. Readers are also informed of other sources of string figures. In addition the book discusses why sharing string figures with students is beneficial for them and what skills they will obtain when they make string figures themselves.

Use of the Book

Read the Basic String Figure Instructions section first and practice the beginning figures. The stories are in approximate order from the easiest to the most difficult. They progress through stories told with one simple figure to stories that use many different figures. The first "story" is only two lines and would work well as a beginning or ending to a traditional storytelling session. "Jack and the Beanstalk" is last, not because the figures are the hardest, but because it is told in rhyme and needs to be retold exactly. The most important thing is to jump right in, practice a lot, and then share what you have learned with children. It's well worth the effort.

Overview and Instructions

1. History of String Figures

No one knows how long string figures have been in existence. Native people all over the world have entertained themselves by making pictures with strings. Sometimes songs, chants, or stories accompanied the string figures. The first written record of a string figure was recorded by Heraklas, a Greek physician who lived around A.D. 100. This figure did not tell a story, but was instead a noose that supported a broken chin. It was made with a circle of string and woven on the hands, as are all other string figures (D'Antoni 90). This contrasts with knots, which are made with a single length of string, not a loop.

It was not until the late 1800s that anthropologists realized string figures, their names and stories, could tell a lot about the people who invented them. They began to try to learn the figures and record them. Before that many observers dismissed them as child's play or even discouraged them as being obscene, since many figures dealt with bodily functions. The native people may also have kept them secret from other people (Abraham 8). In 1898 W.H. Rivers and Alfred C. Haddon visited the Torres Strait and collected 30 examples of string figures. They were the first to try to figure out a system of recording the steps used in making a figure (Ball 9).

Haddon visited the home of Caroline Jayne of Chicago in 1904. Jayne's brother was a colleague of Haddon. Jayne was 31 years old when she met the English anthropologist. Dr. Haddon encouraged Jayne to attend the St. Louis Worlds Exposition in 1904. While there, she collected string figures from various native groups. After the exposition, she researched string figures and also collected some from the American Southwest. Jayne published the first book of string figures in 1906, entitled *String Figures*. Included in the book are 867 illustrations by Mrs. Morris Cotgrave Betts. One can only imagine how all this was accomplished in the days before computers because it was published only two years after Caroline Jayne first began learning about string figures (Meredith 6).

Many of the traditional stories that accompanied string figures have probably been lost. The people collecting the figures often did not speak the language of the native peoples. They could only record the steps of making the actual figure as they watched it being made. Other stories that have been recorded do not make much sense to our modern world. For example, a figure encountered by the author was said to represent an old man squatting to defecate. People laugh at him so he pretends he is only catching grasshoppers (Maude 25).

Each culture named their figures according to that with which they were familiar. Kathleen Haddon told of the Eskimos making pictures of caribou, bears, birds, and other animals, as well as kayaks. The Navajo and Apaches made figures of stars, storms, tipis, coyotes, and rabbits. People in New Guinea made string pictures of headhunters, drums, canoes, palm trees, fish, and crabs. Haddon pointed out you can learn about a culture by the names of their string figures. "String figures picture the things he knows best and is most familiar with" (Haddon 6). The same figure would get a different name, depending on where the people lived and that with which they were familiar. One widely-known figure is variously named "Jacob's Ladder," "The Bridge," and "Fishing Net."

There were some superstitions once associated with string figures. The Eskimos said boys shouldn't play with string figures for fear it would lead them to become entangled with harpoon lines, and that string figures should be made in the autumn so the sun will be caught in the string and winter will be delayed (Ball 16).

At one time the Eskimos cautioned against playing with string figures too much. If you do, the "Spirit of Cat's Cradles" might get you into its power. A crackling noise is heard that tells of the presence of the spirit. You must grab your string and do Opening A over and over in a contest with the spirit (Haddon 6). The story "Totanguak" by Margaret Read MacDonald is included in this collection and tells about this spirit.

String figures can be a useful way of making new friends and communicating with others of different cultures. The U.S. Army advised World War II soldiers and airmen in the South Pacific to take a loop of string with them. If they were downed in the jungle and a native approached, they should get out the string and begin playing Cat's Cradle as a way of communicating (Helfman 12). A. Johnston Abraham was stationed in the mountains bordering Assam and Burma during World War II. He did indeed use string figures to make friends with a young boy there (115).

The International String Figure Association (ISFA) was started in 1978. Its primary goal is to "gather, preserve, and distribute string figure knowledge so that future generations will continue to enjoy this ancient pastime." Many ISFA members have an interest in anthropology. They study where string figures originated and are fascinated by how string figures traveled from one part of the world to another. Other members are attracted by the mathematical possibilities of the figures. Still others are intrigued with the sheer fun of string figures and sharing them.

ISFA members Will Wirt and Mark Sherman visited Navajo reservations in Utah and Arizona in the winter of 1999-2000 to see if people there still knew string figures. They found that many still do. The Navajo believe that string games are a gift from a deity, Spider Woman. Spider Woman also taught the people weaving, braiding, and knot tying (Sherman 187). They also found that the Navajo people still follow the tradition of doing string figures only in the winter. Winter is the period of time between the first snowfall and the first thunder in the spring, when the hibernating animals are awakened. Those who do string games at other times during the year are warned that they will be "struck by lightning, fall off a horse and die, or be urinated upon by spiders" (121). This will happen because "weaving webs (string figures) in the presence of spiders steals the spotlight from these expert weavers" (187). Pregnant woman are also not supposed to do string games (121).

Children and adults are still fascinated by string figures. In these days of video games, computers, and cell phones, stories told with strings are a unique form of entertainment. String stories can draw listeners into the story as they focus on the magic of the string figures.

2. Basic String Figure Instructions

Storyteller Dave Titus (formerly a school librarian) is a wonderful example for those of you just learning string figures. Dave shares that he didn't know any string figures until he was 55. He was looking for something to provide a segue in a storytelling performance. He learned the Mosquito and then the Cup and Saucer. Then he tried the Spider. While visiting a library in Anchorage prior to a storytelling trip to the Inuit, the children's librarian mentioned that the Inuit knew a lot of the figures. She only knew one and told Dave it would be too hard for him to learn quickly. He took that as a challenge and learned it. Since then string figures have been part of his life. Dave has collected string figures from different groups of people during his many trips around the world. He has been invited by the Inuit elders to share string figures with the children in Alaska so the figures won't be forgotten. Dave also has a String Figure Ministry where he uses string figures to share the Christian Gospel.

If you have never done string figures before, or the last time you tried them was in fourth grade, you should start with the basics. First you need a string. You can use any kind of string and tie the ends together, but a knot gets in the way. To make a continuous loop of string without a knot, cut a length of string made from a synthetic fiber such as nylon. A good length is from fingertip to fingertip of your outstretched arms. Place both ends of the string in a flame from a candle or lighter until they melt. Immediately put both ends together. Wait for them to cool, then roll them between your fingertips to make a smooth connection. Another way to melt the ends is to press them down on an electric stove burner set at medium heat (make sure your fingers don't touch the burner).

Braided string holds the figure better and doesn't slip, but it may be difficult to locate. The nylon string that is most often found in hardware or craft stores is twisted, not braided. The advantage of nylon string is that it is inexpensive.

You may also purchase ready-made braided nylon strings in assorted colors at The String Figure Store <http://www.stringfigurestore.com>. Dave Titus, mentioned earlier, owns the store. It is possible to purchase the strings in bulk. Dave hires workers at Goodwill Industries to cut, assemble, and package the strings. They are proud to help Dave and pleased when he comes to tell them where his strings have been delivered. Any string figure book that is currently in print and string figure videotapes can be purchased at The String Figure Store.

The ideal way to learn string figures is from a person who already knows how to do string figures and is standing right next to you with his or her own string. Since most people are not lucky enough to know a string figure expert, we need to have a way of conveying accurate instructions in print. String figure notation has evolved over the years. The notation used in this book is most closely related to that used by the International String Figure Association.

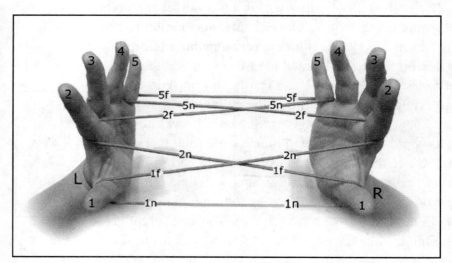

OPENINGALABEL

Each of the fingers is numbered. They are in order, thumb—1, index—2, middle—3, ring—4, and the little finger—5. L stands for left hand and R for right hand. A loop on a finger has two strings, the near string which is closest to you and the far string which is away from you. A small "n" after a finger number indicates the near string on that finger. For example: 2n would be the near string on the index finger. A small "f" indicates the far string. R5f would be the far string on the right little finger.

If the directions indicate an action to be taken by a number without R or L before it, it means you should do that action with that finger on both hands. For example: 2 picks up 5n. That means both index fingers pick up the near string of the little finger loop. But if there is a letter before the number only that finger should do that action. For example: R2 picks up R5n. That means only the right index finger picks up the right near string of the little finger loop.

Other string figure terms:
- Palmar — across the palm.
- Dorsal — across the back of the hand.
- Above — from the side nearest the fingertip.
- Below — from the side nearest the base of the finger.
- Pick up — get string from below on back of finger.
- Hook down — with a finger, grab a string from above. Bend the knuckles and hold the string next the palm.
- Release — take the finger out of the loop.
- Remove — transfer loop from one finger to another.
- Extend — pull the hands apart so the string becomes taut.
- Navajo — slip lower loop over upper loop and release from finger.
- Transverse — a string that goes straight across the hand from one side of a finger to the same side of the finger on the other hand.

Position 1 is a common beginning to many figures. A loop of string is held on both hands. Fingers 1 and 5 of each hand are inside the loop. The string crosses the palm of each hand (the palmar string) *(Illus. Position1)*.

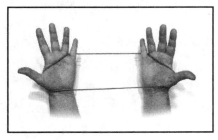

POSITION1

After Position 1, one often moves to Opening A. Begin with Position 1. The index finger on the right hand (R2) crosses over to the left hand, goes under the left palmar string (picks up) *(Illus. OpeningA01)* and pulls back (extends) *(Illus. OpeningA02)*. Between the loop held on R2, the left index finger (L2) picks up the right palmar string and extends. This is Opening A *(Illus. OpeningA)*.

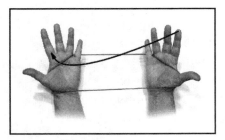

OPENINGA01

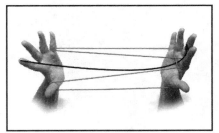

OPENINGA02

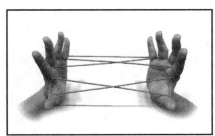

OPENINGA

Witch's Broom or Fish Spear

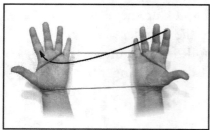

BROOM01

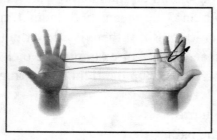

BROOM02

1. Start with Position 1. *(Illus. Broom01)* R2 (the right index finger) picks up the L palmar string.
2. *(Illus. Broom02)* Keeping the string near the fingertip, twist R2 away from you and back three times, creating three twists in the string. Push the loop down on R2.

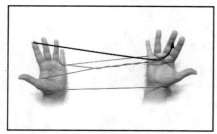

BROOM03

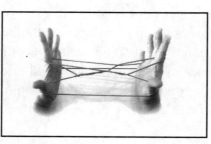

BROOM04

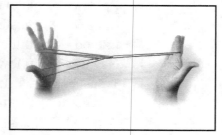

BROOM05

3. *(Illus. Broom03)* L2 (the left index finger) reaches through the R2 loop to pick up R palmar string.
4. *(Illus. Broom04)* Release R1 and R5 and extend *(Illus. Broom05)*.

Navajo Drum

1. Hang the string on one wrist. Bring the other hand into the loop, its fingertips facing the fingertips of the other hand.

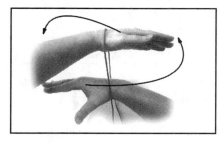

DRUM01

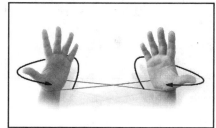

DRUM02

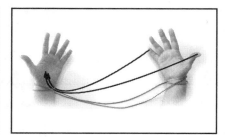

DRUM03

2. *(Illus. Drum01)* Turn your hands up so they are facing each other (this is what it means to return to position). There will be a twist in the loop. (The string shown is shorter than normal.)
3. *(Illus. Drum02)* Your right hand grabs the string on the left wrist closest to you and wraps it counterclockwise around the left wrist. Your left hand grabs the string on the right wrist closest to you and wraps it clockwise around the right wrist.
4. *(Illus. Drum03)* (A normal string is shown.) Your right hand pulls out the string wrapped in front of the left wrist and puts it on the right hand in Position 1. (Thumb and little finger are inside the loop.)

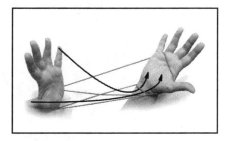

DRUM04

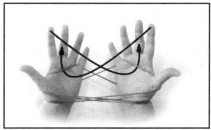

DRUM05

DRUM06

5. *(Illus. Drum04)* Your left hand pulls out the string wrapped in front of the right wrist and put it on the left hand in Position 1.
6. *(Illus. Drum05)* Complete Opening A. (R2 picks up the L palmar string. L2 comes through the R2 loop to pick up R palmar string.) The drum is complete *(Illus. Drum06)*. Hold one hand above the other to display.

Sewing Machine

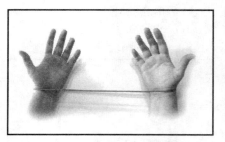

SEWING01

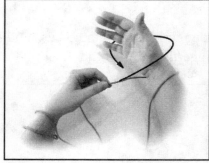

SEWING02

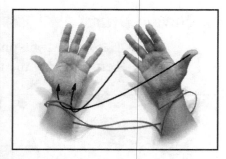

SEWING03

1. Begin with both wrists inside the loop *(Illus. Sewing01)*. (A shorter string than normal is shown.) The right hand grasps the left near wrist string and wraps it counterclockwise around the left wrist.
2. *(Illus. Sewing02)* (Normal string is shown.) The left hand grasps the right far wrist string and wraps it counterclockwise around the right wrist.
3. *(Illus. Sewing03)* The right hand picks up the left wrist string and places it in Position 1 on the right hand.

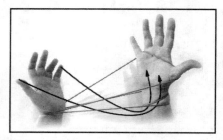

SEWING04

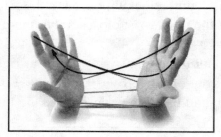

SEWING05

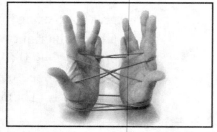

SEWING06

4. *(Illus. Sewing04)* The left hand picks up the right wrist string and places it in Position 1 on the left hand.
5. *(Illus. Sewing05)* Continue with Opening A. (R2 picks up the L palmar string. L2 comes through the R2 loop to pick up R palmar string.)
6. *(Illus. Sewing06)* The right hand reaches around the back of the left hand and picks up the strings and pulls them over the fingers of the left hand. *(Illus. Sewing07)* The left hand picks up the strings on back of the right hand and pulls them over the fingers of the right hand.
7. *(Illus. Sewing08)* Alternate pulling the thumbs further out and then the little fingers. *(Illus. Sewing09)* It will look like a needle pulling thread in and out of fabric.

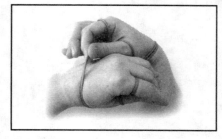

SEWING07

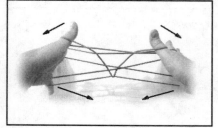

SEWING08

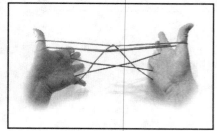

SEWING09

Jacob's Ladder or The Bridge

The instructions are now in strict string figure notation. See if you can do each step using the instructions and then check to see if you have done it correctly by looking at the next illustration. The arrows will show you which string to pick up next.

1. Position A *(Illus. Jacob01)* Release 1.
2. *(Illus. Jacob02)* 1 goes under all strings and picks up 5f. 1 returns to position.
3. *(Illus. Jacob03)* 1 goes over 2n and picks up 2f and returns to position.

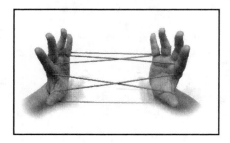

JACOB01

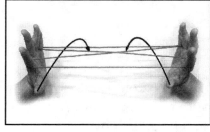

JACOB02

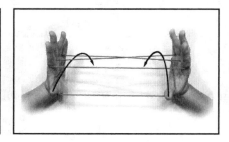

JACOB03

4. *(Illus. Jacob04)* Release loop on 5.
5. *(Illus. Jacob05)* 5 goes over 2n and picks up 1f and returns to position.
6. *(Illus. Jacob06)* Release loops on 1.

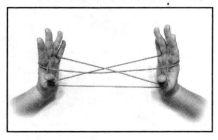

JACOB04

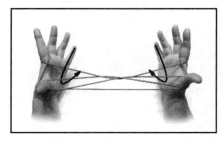

JACOB05

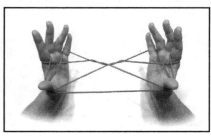

JACOB06

7. *(Illus. Jacob07)* 1 goes over strings on 2 and picks up 5n *(Illus. Jacob08)*.

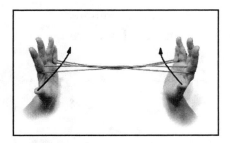

JACOB07

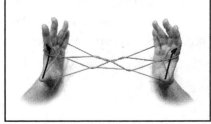

JACOB08

8. R1 and R2 pinch the L2n string closest to the knuckle *(Illus. Jacob09)* and place it over L1. *(Illus. Jacob10)* R1 and R2 pick up the string already on 1 and lift it over the new loop. *(Illus. Jacob11)* This procedure is called Navajoing the loops.

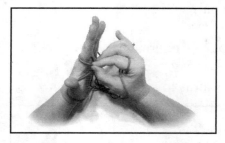

Jacob09

Jacob10

Jacob11

9. Repeat Step 8 on R.
10. *(Illus. Jacob12)* Turn your hands so they're facing toward you. Bend 2 down into the triangles that have formed between 1 and 2. Let the loop come off 5. Point 1 and 2 down and then away from you to form the ladder *(Illus. Jacob13)*.

There are some figures that continue from Jacob's Ladder. Grab the top string of the figure with your teeth. Lower your hands with your thumbs at the bottom. This is the Eiffel Tower *(Illus. Eiffel01)*.

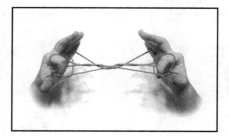

Jacob12

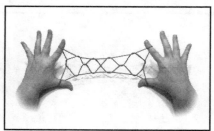

Jacob13

Eiffel01

Still keeping the string in your mouth, release 2 and pull out on 1. This is the Witch's Hat *(Illus. WitchHat01)*.

Make Jacob's Ladder again *(Illus. GrandpaPants00)*. Have a volunteer pull down as indicated while you release 1. Here are Grandpa's Pants, complete with suspenders *(Illus. GrandpaPants01)*.

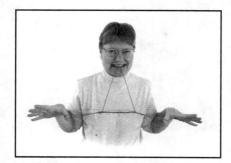

WitchHat01

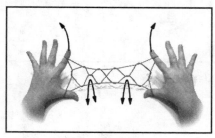

GrandpaPants00

GrandpaPants01

Crocodile Eyes

1. Hang the string behind 2 and 3 on both hands *(Illus. Crocodile01)*. (String shown is shorter than normal.)
2. R1 and R2 pick up string from back of L and pull it through between L2 and L3 *(Illus. Crocodile02)*. Place the string in Position 1 on R. (Normal string is shown.) *(Illus. Crocodile03)*.

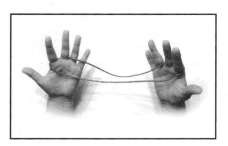

CROCODILE01

CROCODILE02

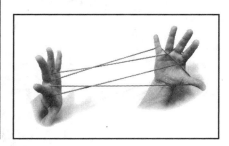

CROCODILE03

3. L1 and L2 pick up the string on the back of R2 and R3 *(Illus. Crocodile04)* and move it to Position 1 on L.
4. *(Illus. Crocodile05)* L2 and L3 tip down over the palmar string into the triangles in front of each of them. L1 and L5 release their loops.
5. *(Illus. Crocodile06)* You might need to lengthen the loops on L2 and L3 by alternately pulling down on them. Remove L2 and L3, leaving the string hanging from R only. L5 enters the R5 loop from above. L5 picks up the R5n string on its back. L1 enters the R1 loop from above. L1 picks up the R1f string on its back.

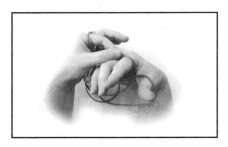

CROCODILE04

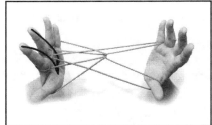

CROCODILE05

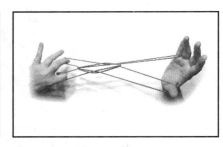

CROCODILE06

6. *(Illus. Crocodile07)* Extend sharply. The crocodile eyes will pop up in the middle of the figure *(Illus. Crocodile08)*.

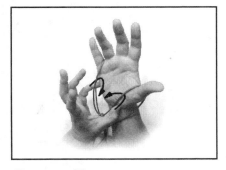

CROCODILE07

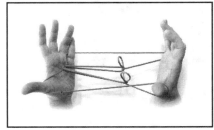

CROCODILE08

Striped Skunk

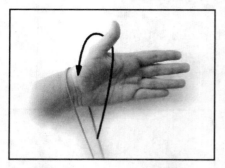

SKUNK01

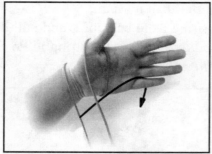

SKUNK02

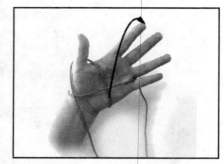

SKUNK03

1. Hang the string on L wrist *(Illus. Skunk01)*. Grasp the far wrist string and hang it on L1 from right to left.
2. *(Illus. Skunk02)* R goes behind the string hanging from L1 and takes the near wrist string. Place it between L4 and L5 so that it hangs behind the hand.
3. *(Illus. Skunk03)* Take the palmar string that is below the string you just moved, pick it up and place it over L2.
4. *(Illus. Skunk04)* Move the string hanging to the left of L1 over L1 so that it hangs down in front of the palm. Move the string hanging to the right of L5 over L5 so that it hangs down in front of the palm.
5. *(Illus. Skunk05)* Lift up the bottom of the long loop hanging from the hand and put it in Position 1 on L. There will now be two loops hanging from L.
6. *(Illus. Skunk06)* R1 enters from below into the loop hanging from L1. R5 enters from below into the loop hanging from L5. Extend.

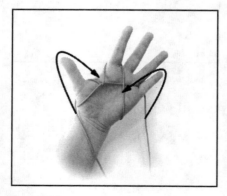

SKUNK04

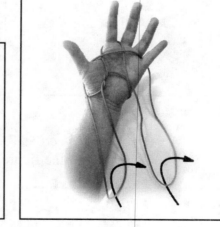

SKUNK05

SKUNK06

7. *(Illus. Skunk07)* Remove the loop from L2 and place it on R2.
8. *(Illus. Skunk08)* Remove the loop from the back of L and bring it in front of L.
9. *(Illus. Skunk09)* Release R2 and extend sharply. The skunk's tail will pop up *(Illus. Skunk10)*. See the stripe down his back?

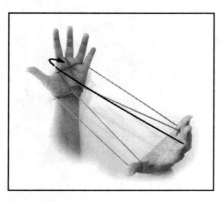

SKUNK07

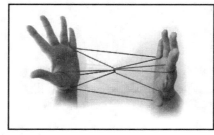

SKUNK08

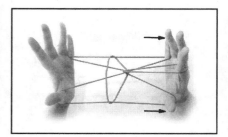

SKUNK09

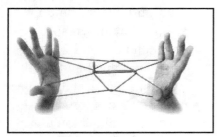

SKUNK10

Mountains and the Sun or Moon.

Kids (and adults) are fascinated by figures that move. Here is a figure that has movement. Dave Titus collected this in Alaska. One of the pilots flying him to a village was a young woman originally from Japan and she showed this figure to him.

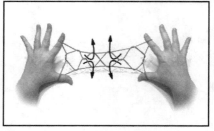

MOUNTAIN01

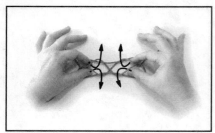

MOUNTAIN02

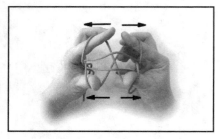

MOUNTAIN03

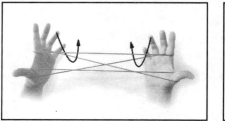

MOUNTAIN04

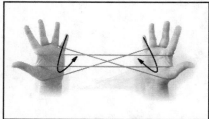

MOUNTAIN05

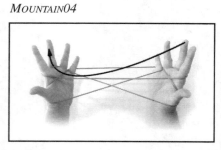

MOUNTAIN06

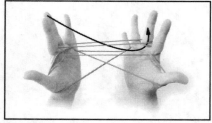

MOUNTAIN07

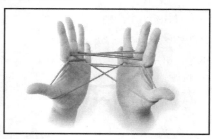

MOUNTAIN08

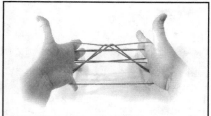

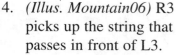

MOUNTAIN09

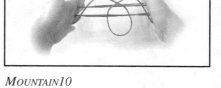

MOUNTAIN10

MOUNTAIN11

1. Begin with Jacob's Ladder *(Illus. Mountain01)*. Lay the figure down. Find the strings that are crossed between the 1 and 2 diamond and the 3 and 4 diamond. Put 1 and 2 on either side of those crossed strings— palms down and fingers facing in *(Illus. Mountain02)*. Bring your fingers back up through the 2 and 3 diamonds *(Illus. Mountain03)*. Extend.
2. *(Illus. Mountain04)* Place 2f so it passes over 4.
3. *(Illus. Mountain05)* 5 picks up 1f.
4. *(Illus. Mountain06)* R3 picks up the string that passes in front of L3.
5. *(Illus. Mountain07)* L3 picks up the string that passes in front of R3.
6. *(Illus. Mountain08)* Release 1.
7. *(Illus. Mountain09)* Release 5 and extend slowly *(Illus. Mountain10)*. The sun or moon will rise until it disappears *(Illus. Mountain11)*.

3. Tips for Performing String Stories

Performing string stories takes practice. It requires some skill to be able to remember the steps of the string figure, talk at the same time, and deal with the nerves of being in front of a group. Some stories include several string figures that can be quite elaborate and require many steps. The best advice is to simply practice, practice, practice. You need to know the string figures well enough that your fingers will automatically do the steps without you consciously thinking about them. Teaching others how to do a figure is one way to learn a figure well.

Try a simple story with one figure first to gain some confidence. If you are a school librarian, you can have the luxury of performing your stories over and over before understanding groups of students. The more you do the stories, the more accomplished you become. It is also helpful to practice in front of a mirror. You will be able to see if there are problems with the way you are displaying the figures.

You may not become a professional storyteller by reading this book, but look for those stories that speak to you and whose string figures you are comfortable performing. Even if you are not a perfect, polished, professional storyteller, there will be many rewards awaiting your storytelling efforts.

A basic thing to remember is to be sure to wear something that contrasts with the color of string you are using. You might choose different colors of strings for different stories. A frog looks best in green! If you find yourself performing string stories frequently, you might even invest in a background screen to make sure the background is not too busy. Be sure to have an extra string with you when you are performing. If a string is going to come apart, inevitably it will happen in the middle of a story.

A string story becomes more than just a story told with string figures when you can add these special touches. A string hangs in just the right position, the actions match the spoken words exactly, and the string becomes an integral part of the story. Add to that the pauses, the volumes, and the excitement of the spoken story and your performance will be truly special and unique. Take the time to learn at least one of these stories and share it with children and adults. You will discover that the language of string figures continues even today.

4. Other Sources of String Figures

The book most often cited whenever anyone discusses string figures is the first one ever published on the subject, Caroline Jayne's *String Figures and How to Make Them*. Originally published in 1906, it is still in print. Anyone interested in string figures should have their own copy of this book. Note that there are a couple of photos in the book of bare-breasted women which might cause laughter among immature children.

The books written by Camilla Gryski are my personal favorites. They are *Cat's Cradles, Owl's Eyes: A Book of String Games, Many Stars & More String Games*, and *Super String Games*. Many of the early sources of string figures contained only written instructions and a picture of the final figure. They are very difficult to follow. Camilla Gryski took those figures, wrote directions that are easy to follow, and included illustrations for every step. She made string figures accessible to all. Unfortunately, her books are now out of print. You may be able to find them in libraries, but if you are truly interested in string figures you'll scramble to purchase your own copies at secondhand bookstores.

Several storytellers contacted for this book said they used the string stories by Anne Pellowski in *The Story Vine*. It was apparent that her stories, published in 1994, have been popular. Her version of "The Farmer and His Yams" is a personal favorite. This book is also out of print, but you will probably find it in a public library or school media center.

Anne Akers Johnson's two string figure books published by Klutz Press are unique because they are spiral-bound board pages which allow them to lay flat while you are learning the figures. They also come with a multicolored string. They do not have a large number of figures, but they are well illustrated.

W. W. Rouse Ball's book *Fun With String Figures* was first published in 1920 and is currently available from Dover Press. It does not contain step-by-step illustrations but includes a lot of interesting information about string figures. *Fun With String* by Joseph Leeming is another reprint from Dover Press. Besides a section on string figures, it also includes string magic, knotting, and braiding.

If you have any interest in learning more about string figures, then you must join the International String Figure Association. For a $25 yearly membership fee, you receive the scholarly journal *Bulletin of the International String Figure Association*, four issues of the *String Figure* magazine, and two newsletters. Many of the research articles contained in the bulletins concern the origin of string figures, their distribution, and theories on how string figures were distributed throughout the world before mass communication. Other articles address the mathematical properties of string figures. The *String Figure* magazines make the membership fee for ISFA a real bargain. Each issue contains the directions for six string figures and are beautifully illustrated. Some figures are from older publications with rewritten directions, some are newly collected from various parts of the world, and others are new creations. *Fascinating String Figures*, published by Dover, is a collection of some of the figures from *String Figure* magazine. You can get information about joining ISFA by visiting their Web page at <http://www.isfa.org> or by sending a letter to International String Figure Association, P. O. Box 5134, Pasadena, California, 91117, USA. The ISFA is also involved in a project called The Arctic String Figure Project. The goal is to rewrite the directions for figures collected over the years from Alaska and

Siberia. Photos and directions are on the Internet for others to test and see if they are easily understood. Eventually these figures will be put in a book. ISFA has a listserv for people interested in string figures. There are not always a lot of messages posted, but it's possible to learn new figures here. There is also a list of Web sites about string figures at the ISFA site. One especially recommended is Richard Darsie's "World-Wide Webs." While it only includes photos of the final figure, it is a very interesting site.

Watching a videotape can be a very good way to learn string figures. Dave Titus's *String Magic* videotape is a good example. As Dave shows you how to do a figure, he repeats the instructions three times. If you still haven't gotten it, you can rewind the tape. Barbara G. Schutzgruber also has a string figure videotape where you can watch her perform string figure stories and learn some figures. David Novak performs his "Jack and the Beanstalk" string story on the *Tell Me A Story Vol. I* videotape.

5. Sharing String Figures with Children

While it is enjoyable to tell string stories to students, it is also rewarding to teach students how to do string figures themselves. In his book originally published in 1920, Ball talks about sharing string figures. "These figures, when shown to a few spectators in a room, always prove, as far as my experience goes, interesting alike to young and old; but their attractiveness, their fascination I might always say, is not permanent unless people can be induced to construct them for themselves" (2).

If you are a school librarian, you have a unique relationship with the children in your building. You see the children on a regular basis and then continue to see them every year. You can do a story time that includes string stories. But unlike a professional storyteller who is there once, you have the opportunity to continue sharing with students over an extended period of time. Because of this you can teach children to do the figures themselves. It is great to see the looks on children's faces when they master a figure for the first time. It is special to see a child patiently teaching a fellow student how to do a figure. A kindergartner will show she can do Jacob's Ladder, and you know her brother took the time to teach her. Generations discover they share a common interest when a child learns that Mom or Dad or Grandpa knows a string figure.

Students gain many skills when they learn string figures. Sequencing is especially enhanced by string figures. Students must follow a sequence exactly or the figure will not appear. Students become more proficient at giving exact directions when they teach their classmates new figures. String figures are good for developing the small muscles in the hands. They are an engaging activity, involving memory and motor skills. Students develop confidence from being able to learn complicated figures and then share them with their classmates. They are proud of themselves for learning a new skill.

You will likely find that when string figures are first introduced to a school, they become a very popular activity. Recess and bus rides are natural times for students to do string figures. It's probably a good idea to stress that strings should not be out in classrooms unless teachers have given permission. Always stress to students that they should never wear a string around their neck because they could be injured if the string were to become caught on something.

When teaching string figures to students, it is desirable that every student successfully complete one figure. Children can be given strings and told they are practice strings that they will be giving back at the end of the period, so it doesn't matter what color they get. You will find that some students will be successful the first time you teach the figure and they can help the others. Teachers and other adults can also be called on to help. One way to be sure that all students are successful is to have students who have finished the figure sit down so you know who still needs help.

Dave Titus does school residencies that include introducing students to string figures. He likes to teach a different figure to each class or grade level and then asks the students to teach other students. By the end of his time at a school, most students know several figures. If students become frustrated and say they can't do it Titus reminds them that they don't know how to do it— yet. They need to keep trying until they do get it. He tells students that if it was easy it wouldn't be that much fun. Titus' philosophy is that we are proud of ourselves when we finally can do something that is hard and we shouldn't give up.

It is interesting to see children interact as they teach each other to do figures. It is exciting when you see children willingly stop what they are doing to help a fellow student who wants to learn a new figure.

It is challenging for two students to do a figure together. One student provides the right hand and the other the left. It's interesting how a figure done with your own two hands becomes a different challenge when you are only providing one of the hands.

Students can be encouraged to make up their own stories to go with a figure or a series of figures. Carlita Beltz, third grade teacher at Rivermont Collegiate School in Bettendorf, Iowa, introduces her children to string figures during a unit on the westward movement in the United States. While she is not certain that children traveling the Oregon Trail did string figures, she feels it is logical to believe they may have entertained themselves with a piece of string, as did other people from around the world. Carlita invites former students to come help teach some figures. Then her students are given the assignment to pretend they are sitting with their families and other travelers around a campfire. They have to tell a story with string figures. On one day the students dress up as pioneers and they share their stories.

You could make a large string figure through a group effort. A large string could be made of thin rope and students would represent individual fingers. A string figure troupe could do performances at area libraries, other schools, hospitals, and nursing homes. String figures can be very therapeutic and engaging for people of all ages. And wouldn't it be fun to use a neon string and perform with a black light…? The possibilities are endless.

The Witch's Broom, Navajo Drum, and Sewing Machine are easy figures to teach whole classes of children. The instructions were given in the second part of this chapter. The following hints are specifically for teaching students to do string figures.

Here's an easy way to tell children to get the string in Position 1. "Put your thumbs into the loop and pull out as far as you can. Make sure there isn't a twist in the loop. Then slide your little fingers up into the loop next to your thumbs. Hold your hands so they are facing each other. That's Position 1."

Kindergarteners, as well as older students can successfully do Witch's Broom as detailed previously. For students who are having trouble twisting the string by themselves in Step 2, take the string on the right index finger and twist it around their finger for them. Stand beside the students. When they begin Step 4, have them put their left hand on the bottom and their right hand on the top. Hold onto all of their left hand fingers with your right hand so none of the loops will fall off. You can hold onto the right index finger with your left hand to keep that loop from falling off. Have them drop the loops off their thumb and little finger of the right hand. You help keep the loops in the right places and their first string figure appears right before their eyes.

Another figure that students can do is Cut Your Hand. It does require two people so it can take more time for all students to do it once.
1. Opening A
2. *(Illus. Cut01)* Ask a volunteer to insert their hand from above into the fig-ure between L2 and R2.
3. *(Illus. Cut02)* Release 2 and 5.
4. *(Illus. Cut03)* Put 5 back into loop as in Position 1. Do Opening A again.

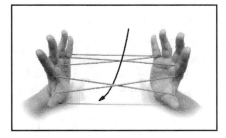
CUT01

CUT02

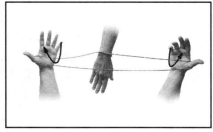
CUT03

5. *(Illus. Cut04)* Instruct volunteer to insert their hand from below into the figure between L2 and R2.
6. *(Illus. Cut05)* Release 2 and 5. At the same time pull hands apart quickly. The string will appear to pass through the wrist of the volunteer.

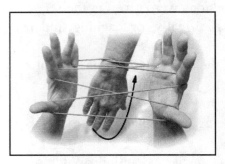

Cut04

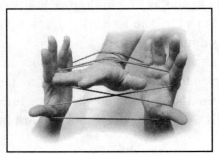

Cut05

For very young children you can grab onto their thumbs when you instruct them to drop the string from their index and little fingers in Step 3. You can do that even if you're the one getting your hand cut off; just cross your hands—your right hand grabs their right thumb and your left hand grabs their left thumb. Hang on until the other loops have been dropped.

It is very important that if the left palmar string is picked up first in Step 1 it must be picked up first in Step 4. Otherwise the trick will not work. At this step you can hold onto the thumbs of the student again to make sure the string does not fall off.

If you have a very young child who would like to participate but is too young to do a figure, you can have them be the volunteer and cut off their hand. You may have to reassure them that you promise not to really cut off their hand.

Students enjoy the Jacob's Ladder figure but many find the last step to be difficult. Kids can get the strings twisted in all sorts of ways. It is helpful to keep telling them to point down, down, down while spreading thumbs and index fingers apart.

The rest of the figures in the second part of this chapter are ones that children enjoy learning. While they are not as easy to teach in a large group, you might teach them to a small group of students and encourage them to teach their friends.

Safety Notice: Remind students to never wear a string around their necks.

The Stories

1. "The Balloon" by Dorothy Gruber

This story would make a good beginning or end to story time.

1.   *Hang the loop over L2 and L3 so the strings hang in front of the palm (A shorter string than usual is shown.) (Illus. Balloon01).*

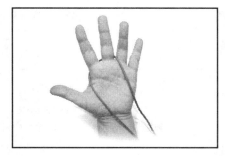

BALLOON01

2.   *R goes into the loop hanging in front of L from underneath (Illus. Balloon02).*

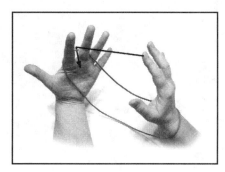

BALLOON02

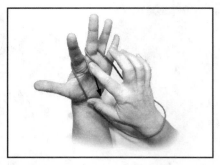

BALLOON03

3. R2 goes in the space between L2 and L3 and hooks down on the string behind those fingers (Illus. Balloon03).

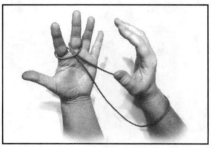

BALLOON04

4. R2 pulls this string out as far as it will go. The loop that was on R will move up to cross in front of R2 and R3. R goes into hanging loop from underneath (Illus. Balloon04).

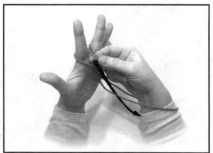

BALLOON05

5. R1 and R2 grab the 2f and 3n strings together above the crossing string, closest to the fingers (Illus. Balloon05). Make sure that the loops do not get twisted as you pull them back through the loop on R (Illus. Balloon06).

BALLOON06

6. *Put R3, R4, and R5 into the loop held by R2. This will make the loop wider. There are two strings on the top and two strings on the bottom of this loop. L1 takes the bottom near string and L5 takes the bottom far string (Illus. Balloon07). Release the loops from R (Illus. Balloon08).*

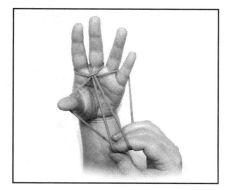

BALLOON07

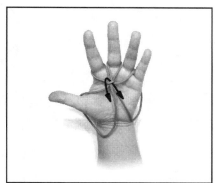

BALLOON08

You now have a balloon ready for flight. We wish you gentle winds and soft landings.

Notes: Gryski (*Cat's Cradle* 34) says this figure is The Hogan, a Navajo tent. When the fingers of the left hand are removed it is A Bunch of Bananas. Ball names it A Frame Work for a Hut and thinks that upside-down it might look like a parachute (27). Abraham says it is called The Grass Hut in Central Africa (49). He also notes it looks like a parachute.

7. *There is a small loop that goes around the strings on L2 and L3. R1 and R2 pick it up and pull it out gently (Illus. Balloon09).*

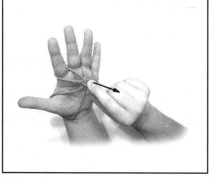

BALLOON09

8. *Tip the hands so that L is on top and R on the bottom (normal string is shown.) (Illus. Balloon10).*

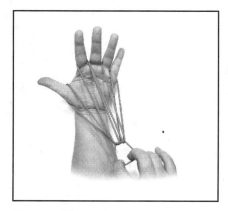

BALLOON10

2. "Saving the Princess" by Philip Noble

Philip Noble of Scotland, a founding member of the IFSA, wrote this story. Some additional details have been suggested by Udo Engelhardt from Germany.

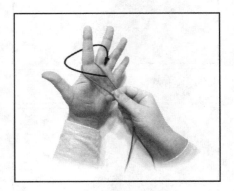

PRINCESS01

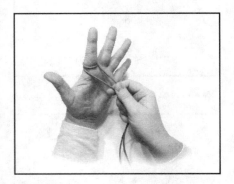

PRINCESS02

PRINCESS03

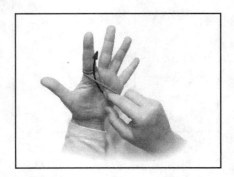

PRINCESS04

1. *Hang a loop over L2.*

2. *(Illus. Princess01) Take the far string and twist it clockwise around L2.*

3. *(Illus. Princess02) Pull at the hanging loop with your right hand but in a way that the double loop at L2 does not come off.*

4. *(Illus. Princess03) Hold the hanging loop between R1 and R345 and make sawing motion with R2 on the two strings coming from L2. R2 moves under L2, then into the space between the two strings from below, up and then over L2.*

5. *(Illus. Princess04) And then around it again into the space between the strings from below (Illus. Princess05).*

Once upon a time there was a kingdom with a beautiful princess, but… there was also a bad wizard in that kingdom. The wizard captured the princess and tied her with a magic rope

and closed her up in his basement. Her father, the king, sent the strongest men in his kingdom to free her, and they pulled at the rope as hard as they could

in vain because the rope was a magic rope! Then the king sent his knights and they tried to cut the rope with their swords

in vain again because the rope was a magic rope.

Then came a young man who lived in the village, and he asked, "May I come in?" The princess answered in a sobbing voice "Yes, please, come in!" He entered the basement.

Then he asked the beautiful princess, "Oh, you look so sad, may I give you a kiss?" Sobbing again the princess answered, "Yes, you may." Then the young man gave her a kiss

and, O wonder! the rope came off!

Together they walked back to the castle. The king was so pleased the young man had saved his daughter that he gave her hand to him in marriage. And so they lived happily ever after.

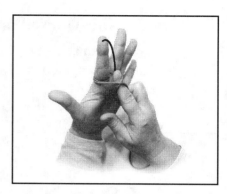

PRINCESS05

6. *R2 and L2 come together at their fingertips (Illus. Princess06).*

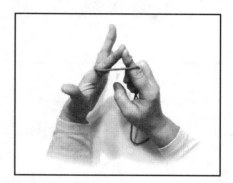

PRINCESS06

7. *Release R345 holding the two strings and the string will come off (Illus. Princess07).*

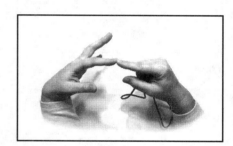

PRINCESS07

Note: Philip Noble likes to wrap the string around the thumb of another person. He then holds the strings with his left hand. His left arm is used as a "road" for the right fist to "walk" along as the soldiers and knights come to try to save the princess. The movements of the right hand are the same when the young man kisses the princess and the string falls off.

This trick was included in the March 2001 *String Figure* magazine. It is called Burmese Slip Trick and was collected by Abraham in Burma.

The following three stories are told with the same figure.

3. "The Mouse Family" by Norma J. Livo

"The Mouse Family" was written for Storytellers International™ by Norma J. Livo and copyrighted in 1993.

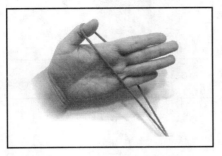

ORANGE01

1. Hold your left hand with the fingers pointing to the right. Hang the loop over L1 with a string hanging in front of the hand (palmar string) and a string hanging in the back (dorsal string) (Illus. Orange01).

Once there was a family of mice.

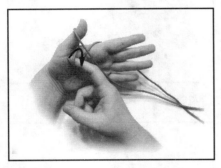

ORANGE02

2. (Illus. Orange02) Going under the palmar string, R2 enters the space between L1 and L2. R2 hooks down on the dorsal string and pulls a short loop to the palm of the hand.

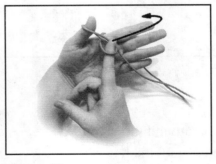

ORANGE03

3. (Illus. Orange03) Twist R2 a half turn clockwise.

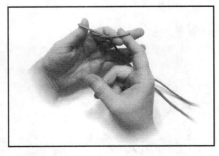

ORANGE04

4. (Illus. Orange04) Place the loop on L2.

There was a father mouse. Father mouse had long whiskers and a sharp nose.

5. *(Illus. Orange 05) Pull both strings hanging from the hand to tighten the loop on L2.*

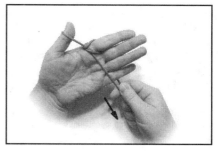

ORANGE05

6. *(Illus. Orange06) Going under the palmar string, R2 enters the space between L2 and L3. R2 hooks down on the dorsal string and pulls a short loop to the palm of the hand.*

7. *Twist R2 a half turn clockwise. Place the loop on L3.*

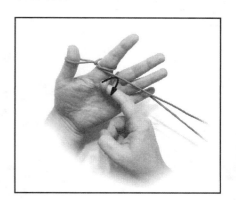

ORANGE06

Mother mouse had pink ears and shiny eyes

8. *(Illus. Orange07) Pull on both hanging strings to tighten.*

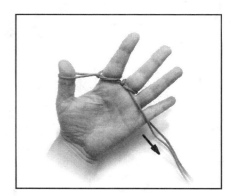

ORANGE07

9. *(Illus. Orange08) Going under the palmar string, R2 enters the space between L3 and L4. R2 hooks down on the dorsal string and pulls a short loop to the palm of the hand.*

10. *Twist R2 clockwise and place the loop on L4.*

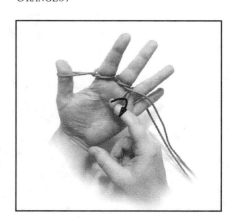

ORANGE08

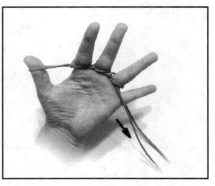

11. *(Illus. Orange09) Pull on both hanging strings to tighten.*

12. *Going under the palmar string, R2 enters the space between L4 and L5. R2 hooks down on the dorsal string and pulls a short loop to the palm of the hand.*

while the girl mouse had a nose that twitched as she walked.

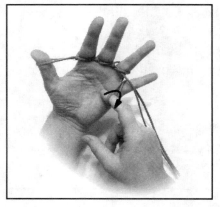

ORANGE10

13. *(Illus. Orange10) Twist R2 clockwise and place the loop on L5.*

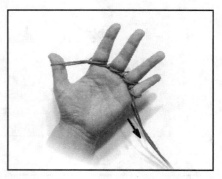

ORANGE11

14. *(Illus. Orange11) Pull on both hanging strings to tighten.*

The boy mouse had dirty feet from walking in the mud.

They came upon a piece of cheese near the hole in the wall they lived in. Quietly all four mice tiptoed to the cheese and just as they were ready for a feast, the cat jumped out at them. They all scurried back to the safety of the hole, squeaking loudly as they ran.

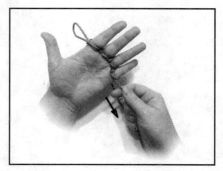

ORANGE12

15. *Remove L1 from loop (Illus. Orange12). Quickly pull only the palmar string from where it is hanging at the bottom of the hand. The loops will disappear from the hand.*

4. "Old Man Coyote and the Little Rabbit" by Esther Martinez (Blue Water)

Esther Martinez (Blue Water) of San Juan Pueblo wrote this story. It was shared by Storytellers International™.

A little rabbit once lived at Póshu? Póyâadi in San Juan Pueblo. He always had to outsmart Old Man Coyote, for rabbit is a coyote's favorite dish.

One night Coyote caught Rabbit by the water. Rabbit said, "Why eat me when I am keeping some cheese cool for you in the water?" Coyote, thinking the reflection of the half moon was cheese, took Rabbit's advice; he placed a leaf on the water to step on to reach the cheese. Of course, he tumbled into the water and the current carried him along. Meanwhile, Rabbit escaped.

Coyote grabbed some willows, pulled himself out, stretched out in the warm sun to recover and fell asleep.

> *Place string over hand as in Step 1 in the previous story,*
> *"The Mouse Family."*

While he was asleep the frogs cut all his hair, snip-snip-snip-snip.

> *Weave the string over all the fingers, Steps 2 through 14.*

When he woke, he stood up and began to shake himself. Every time he shook, more hair fell off until it was all gone.

> *Release your thumb and pull the palmar string (Step 15) so*
> *that the string is removed from one finger at a time.*

He asked everyone in the pueblo, "Who cut off my hair?" but everyone shrugged and said, "I don't know. I was busy."

So Old Man Coyote went off crying to White Sand, and left little Rabbit behind still leaving tracks along the Rio Grande.

5. "The Orange Mouse" by Audrey Collinson Small

Audrey Small grew up in England where her mother was very interested in string figures. Audrey has continued this family tradition and often writes poems to go with string figures.

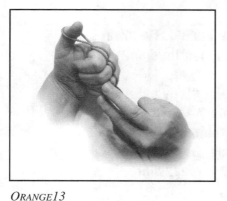

ORANGE13

Slowly make Steps 1 through 14 of the figure in "The Mouse Family."

Make a fist with L. Walk your R fingers up the knuckles of L (Illus. Orange13).

In our house
  there's a room
    at the top
      of the stairs.

On Hallowe'en Night
  go up there
    who dares.

ORANGE14

Withdraw L1 from its loop. R1 and R2 help to untwist the loop. Hold it in place with L1 at the base to show a little pumpkin (Illus. Orange14).

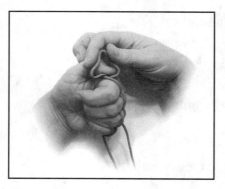

ORANGE15

Pull up the loop, squeezing the top of it with R1 and R2 to make a witch's hat (Illus. Orange15).

He won't find a pumpkin

or even a witch

but he will find a mouse

with a tail that goes
SWISH!

This mouse isn't gray.

This mouse isn't brown.

It's a mouse you won't find

everywhere around town.

It's ORANGE this mouse

and it lives in our house.

But on All Hallow's Day

it SCAMPERS AWAY!

Make the mouse's ears by holding down the witch's hat with L1. Make the mouse's tail swish by holding with R (Illus. Orange16).

Move L from side to side as if saying no.

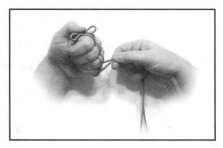

ORANGE16

Pull hard on hanging palmar string so string falls away from hand.

Notes: You'll want to use an orange string, of course. This story works well with a small group of children gathered around you or with one on your lap.

This figure is well known. It is often called The Mouse or the Yam Thief. It has been associated with many different stories. Storyteller Anne Pellowski, in her collection of stories *The Story Vine*, says that a Japanese librarian told her she knew it from childhood as Train. "As each loop was put on the fingers, a car was added to the train, starting with the engine and ending with the caboose. When it was time for the train to move on, the engineer got up steam (the loop was taken off the left thumb) and slowly the train chugged off, making the 'cars' disappear one by one into the tunnel" (9).

Abraham says this figure is probably the most widely distributed of all releases (23). (A release is where the string is wrapped around the fingers. It looks impossible to remove it quickly, but pulling on one string is all it takes.)

Ball's version says that the thumb loop is the owner of a yam patch who is sleeping. The other loops represent bags of yams dug up by a thief and ready to be carried off. The owner wakes up, sees the bags of yams, and looks for the thief (7).

Pellowski's version of this story, "The Farmer and His Yams" is widely used (9).

6. "My Cow"—String Figures by Axel Reichert

This is an original series of figures called Alpine Cow by Axel Reichert of Germany. It was published in the September 2001 issue of *String Figure* magazine.

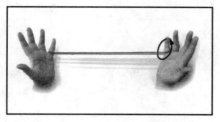

Cow01

1. *Place loop on 5. (Illus. Cow01). (A shorter string than usual is shown.) Twist R5 once away from you.*

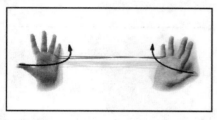

Cow02

2. *(Illus. Cow02) 1 picks up 5n.*

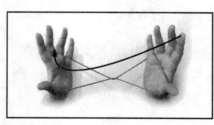

Cow03

3. *(Illus. Cow03) R2 picks up L palmar string.*

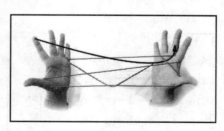

Cow04

4. *(Illus. Cow04) L2 picks up R palmar string between strings on R2. (Normal string is shown.)*

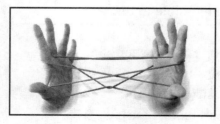

Cow05

5. *(Illus. Cow05) Turn fingers away from you. Hold hands with L on bottom and R on top.*

Ding dong! Ding dong! Do you hear the bell?

6. *(Illus. Cow06) Twist hands from side to side so that 1n and 5f strings move from side to side. This is the clapper of the bell (Illus. Cow07).*

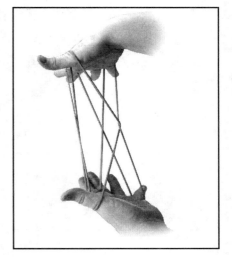

Cow06

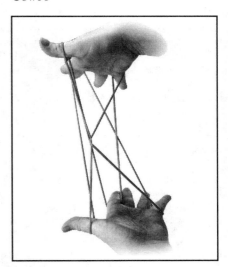

Cow07

7. *(Illus. Cow08) Return the hands to position. Pull hands apart so that 5f pulls straight across and the 1n string hooks over it. 1 passes over 2 loop and 5n to pick up the string that hooks over 5f. L1 picks up the left section of this string before it hooks over 5f and R1 picks up the right section of this string.*

8. *(Illus. Cow09) 1 returns to position. Navajo the loops on 1.*

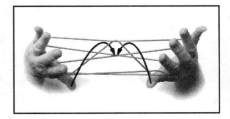

Cow08

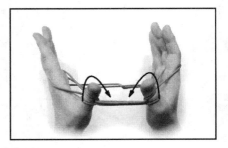

Cow09

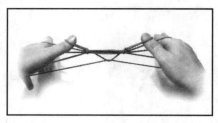

Cow10

9. *(Illus. Cow10) Extend and pull so that knots form.*

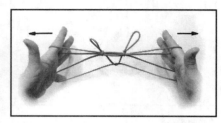

Cow11

10. *(Illus. Cow11) Release 1. You may need to pull back on 2 to form the face of the cow.*

It's just my cow Bessie

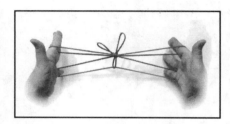

Cow12

11. *Continue pulling on 2 until knots come together and the three leaves of clover forms (Illus. Cow12).*

coming to eat her clover!

7. "Clown King: A Cat's Cradle Tale" by Audrey Collinson Small

Audrey has written articles for the *Bulletin of the International String Figure Association*. She is pleased that others are interested in string figures, too.

There lived a king

who wore his crown

1. Position 1 (Illus. Crown01) Lift your hands up as if to display the king's domain.

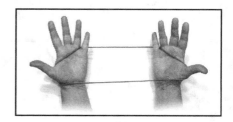

CROWN01

whenever he could

2. Opening A (Illus. Crown02). Keep the loops on 2 near the fingertips. Hold the figure over your head.

upside down.

3. 1 picks up 2n.

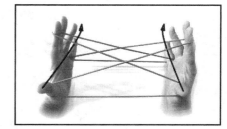

CROWN02

4. (Illus. Crown03) Navajo the loops on 1.

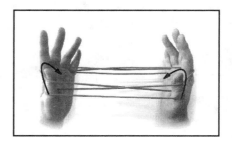

CROWN03

5. (Illus. Crown04) Drop 5 (Illus. Crown05).

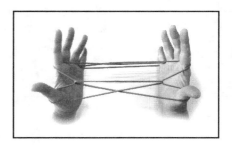

CROWN04

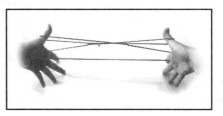

CROWN05

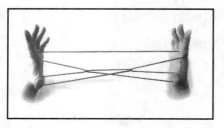

CROWN06

6. *Turn the figure up so it turns into the cup and saucer (Illus. Crown06). Pretend to slurp some tea.*

At 4 o'clock he slurped his tea

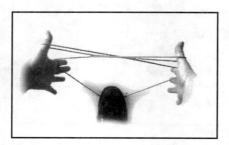

CROWN07

7. *Turn figure upside down again. With your foot, step onto 2n string (Illus. Crown07).*

dumped the rest

CROWN08

8. *Release 2. Alternate pulling up each side so that king climbs the tree (Illus. Crown08).*

and climbed a tree.

9. *Release loop from foot. L1 removes R1 from above (Illus. Crown09). L2 helps to hold the loops in place on L1 (Illus. Crown10).*

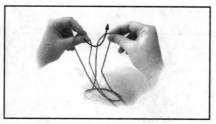

CROWN09

10. *R1 and R2 grab the string and the loop around the strings hanging from L1 (Illus. Crown11). Pull down in a smooth movement to show the king sliding on down.*

At supper time he slid on down.

The king who liked to play the clown.

Note: This series of figures is Small's invention.

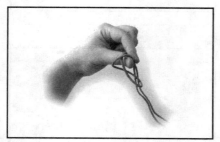

CROWN10

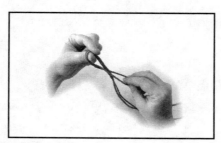

CROWN11

8. "The Cat and the Mice" by Aesop

Axel Reichert collected this string series of figures from a Nigerian man who was visiting Germany. It was published in the December 2000 issue of *String Figure* magazine.

Gwyn Calvetti suggested this story to go with this figure.

There once was a house that was overrun with mice. A cat

1. *(Illus. Mouse01) Opening A. 4, over 2 loop, removes 1 loop from above.*

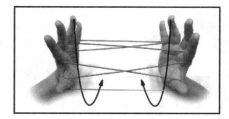

MOUSE01

2. *(Illus. Mouse02) 5, through 4 loop from above, picks up its own 5n string.*

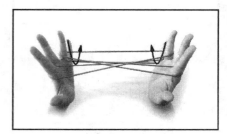

MOUSE02

3. *(Illus. Mouse03) Navajo the loops on 5.*

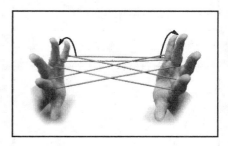

MOUSE03

learned of this, and said to herself, "That sounds like a great opportunity for me," and she went off to live in that house. She caught the mice one by one and ate them.

4. *(Illus. Mouse04) Release 2 and extend sharply. Grab the middle strings in your teeth, turn your hands over, and gesture as if you have claws.*

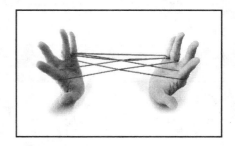

MOUSE04

The poor remaining mice finally gave up and they decided to go to their holes and stay here.

5. *(Illus. Mouse05) 1 picks up all the strings.*

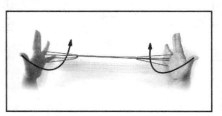

MOUSE05

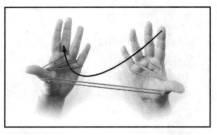

MOUSE06

6. (Illus. Mouse06) R2 picks up the lowest L palmar string.

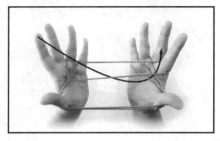

MOUSE07

7. (Illus. Mouse 07) L2, through the R2 loop, picks up the lowest R palmar string.

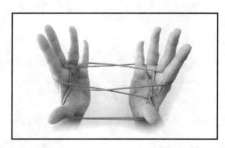

MOUSE08

8. (Illus. Mouse08) Release 5 and 1. Extend gently, pointing fingers away from you.

Of course the cat was disappointed she could no longer get to the mice. She spent some time trying to figure out a way to trick the mice and get them to come out of their holes again. Finally she climbed up on the wall and hung from a peg, pretending to be dead.

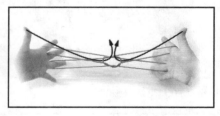

MOUSE09

9. (Illus. Mouse09) Then 1 picks up the side of the middle circle closest to it.

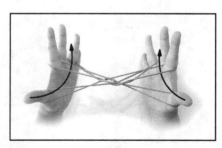

MOUSE10

10. (Illus. Mouse10) 1 picks up 2n.

11. *(Illus. Mouse11) Navajo the loops on 1.*

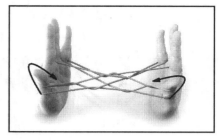

MOUSE11

After a while a mouse peeped out and saw the cat hanging there. "So," it cried, "you think you're quite smart, don't you? You may look dead but we are still not going to come near you!"

The moral of this story is: Do not let yourself be tricked by a known enemy.

12. *(Illus. Mouse12) Release 2 and extend gently with fingers pointing away from you (Illus. Mouse13).*

MOUSE12

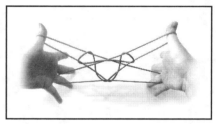

MOUSE13

Notes: Many of us call the first figure Crow's Feet. It is a figure with many names. Jayne says it is known as The Leashing of Lochiel's Dogs, along with Tying Dogs Feet, Duck's Feet, and a Wooden Spoon (116). The man from Nigeria who showed the figure to Axel Reichert called it Fufu Stick which is a pestle used to pound African yams or cassava roots. You can find another way to make Crow's Feet in the "Going Fishing" story on page 86. The second figure in the series is one from Nigeria called Moon. The third figure was not named by the Nigerian man but Axel thinks it looks like a famous mouse.

9. "African Bat" as told by Valerie Baadh

Valerie Baadh (pronounced *Bothe*, to rhyme with *clothe*) is a movement specialist and the games and physical education teacher at the San Francisco Waldorf School. She states that although the folktale, "Why the Bat Flies At Night" does not traditionally accompany this figure, both are indigenous to West Africa. Valerie indicates this is a good story to tell at the beach or during sandal weather.

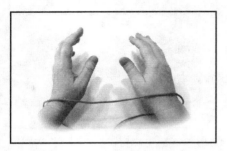

BAT01

1. *Hang the string on the wrists of both hands. The string should hang in a long loop (Illus. Bat01).*

Long ago, the Bat flew in the daylight. But the Bat's mother became sick, and the wise Antelope said that only the sun could help her.

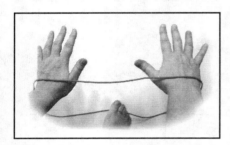

BAT02

2. *Catch the bottom of the loop with your big toe (Illus. Bat02).*

So the Bat asked the sun to cure his mother but the sun said, "No!" He was too busy.

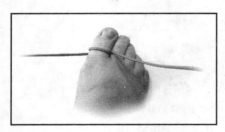

BAT03

3. *Taking the right string, wrap string once clockwise around the big toe (Illus. Bat03).*

And she died.

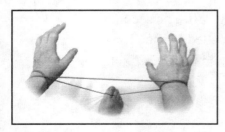

BAT04

4. *Turn your hands out toward the sides, then rotate them down and around the string. The string will wrap once around each wrist (Illus. Bat04).*

The Bat asked the animals to help bury his mother, but the animals said, "No! You are not our kin. You fly like a bird!"

So the Bat asked the birds to help bury his mother, but the birds said, "No! You are not our kin. You have no feathers!"

So, he buried his mother alone.

Since that day the Bat never again flew by the light of the sun, but only in darkness.

5. *1 and 2 of both hands reach down and pick up the top of the string looped around the big toe. Pull it up (Illus. Bat05).*

BAT05

6. *Pull the toe loop up with L2 and R2 and at the same time let the wrist loops drop off the wrists (Illus. Bat06).*

7. *Adjust the shape by pulling on the bat's wings. Move the strings up and down to make the bat fly.*

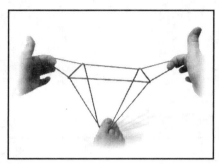

BAT06

10. "The Sardines," A Traditional Tale

This figure is found in *String Figures from New Caledonia and the Loyalty Islands* (26-27).

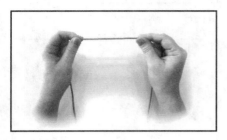

SARDINES01

1. *(Illus. Sardines01) Hold a short portion of the string between your hands.*

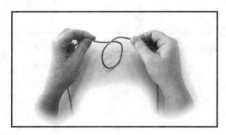

SARDINES02

2. *(Illus. Sardines02) Form a small loop.*

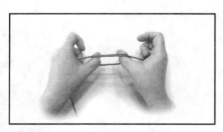

SARDINES03

3. *(Illus. Sardines03) Insert 1 into this loop from the front.*

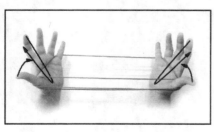

SARDINES04

3. *(Illus. Sardines04) Release the rest of the fingers. Insert 5 into the larger loop that is hanging down and extend. There will be two 1n strings, one 1f string, and one 5f string.*

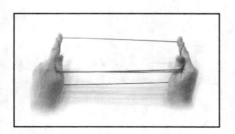

SARDINES05

4. *(Illus. Sardines05) 2 enters 1 loop from below, picks up 1f on its tip. 1 presses into the side of 2 to keep strings from slipping off. Turn hands away from you to display. 3, 4, 5 can turn down on 5f to keep it taut. This is the Caroline Extension.*
5. *Remove 1.*

A fisherman came to the sea one day to catch some sardines. The sea was calm and he did not see any fish.

6. (Illus. Sardines06) 1 goes under all strings and brings back 5f and 5n on its back. 1 goes into 2 loop from below.

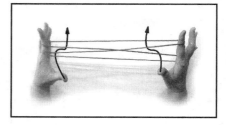

SARDINES06

7. (Illus. Sardines07) 1 hooks down on 2f, turns away from you and returns to position.

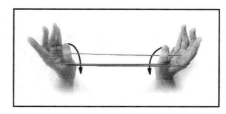

SARDINES07

8. (Illus. Sardines075) Release 2.

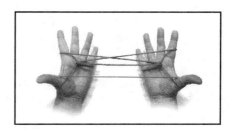

SARDINES075

9. (Illus. Sardines08) 1 picks up 5n.

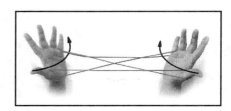

SARDINES08

Then he saw two sardines. But he was greedy and decided to wait for more.

10. (Illus. Sardines09) Caroline Extension. Two fish will form (Illus. Sardines10).

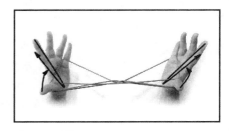

SARDINES09

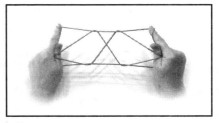

SARDINES10

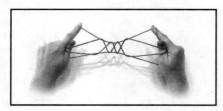

SARDINES11

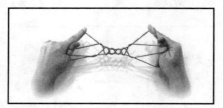

SARDINES12

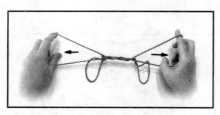

SARDINES13

11. *Repeat Steps 5 through 10. Four fish will form (Illus. Sardines11).*

12. *Repeat Steps 5 through 10 yet again. Six fish will form (Illus. Sardines12).*

17. *Remove 1. Release 2 (Illus. Sardines13).*

18. *Extend and figure dissolves.*

Then there were four sardines. Still the fisherman waited for more.

Then there were six sardines swimming in the sea. Just as the fisherman decided it was time for him to catch the fish, two bigger fish came swimming up

and ate up all the sardines.

The fisherman went home without any sardines.

11. "Totanguak" by Margaret Read MacDonald

This story was included in the book *When the Lights Go Out: Twenty Scary Stories* by Margaret Read MacDonald.

Many Eskimo children are expert at string figures. There is even a string figure spirit, named Totanguak, who lurks outside at night hoping to find some child who will wake up and play with him. If you play string figure games with Totanguak and he wins, the spirit will take you away with him forever.

There once was an Eskimo boy who lived with his father in an igloo.
One evening when his father was asleep the boy woke up.
He didn't want to go back to sleep.
Instead, he took out his string and began to play string figures.

First he made the figure of the polar bear.
Then he made the figure of the Northern Star.
Then he made his favorite figure ... the falling down tent.
As the boy made the tent
he told himself the story of how a snowstorm came suddenly
and broke down the tent.
The two little boys inside ran away in opposite directions.
All this was acted out in the string figure.

The little boy was having a fine time playing string figures.
Suddenly he felt as if there were someone else inside the igloo.
He looked around ...
there by the entrance a man was sitting.

"Hello," said the man.
"I see you like to play string figures.
Could I play with you?"

The little boy was pleased to have someone to play with.
"See ... I have my own string," said the man.

He pulled out his long string.

Pull out your string.

"Let's have a contest and see who can make the string figures the fastest."

"All right," said the little boy.

This boy knew many string figures and could make them very rapidly.

"I'll name the first figure we shall make," said the man.

"Go ahead."

"The figure we will make is ... *The Polar Bear.*"

The little boy knew this one.
He began quickly to weave the string on this fingers.
But already the man had finished!

"You are good at this!" said the little boy.

"Oh ... I know a string figure or two," said the man.

"Well it's my turn to name the string figure we shall make next," said the little boy.
"Let's make ... *The Falling Down Tent.*"

The little boy knew this figure very well.

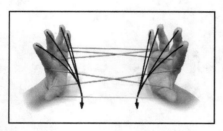

TOTANG01

1. *(Illus. Totang01) Opening A 2, 3, 4, 5 of both hands go down into the 1 loop.*

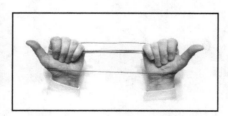

TOTANG02

2. *(Illus. Totang02) The thumb string is flipped over the backs of both hands.*

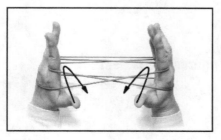

TOTANG03

3. *(Illus. Totang03) 1 goes over the loop that goes around the back of the hands, under all the other strings and hooks up the far hand loop string. 1 returns to its position.*

4. *(Illus. Totang04) R1 and R2 take the string on the back of L and lift it carefully over the other strings. Repeat on R. Pull the hands apart and display the tent.*

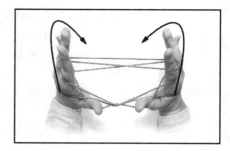

TOTANG04

5. *(Illus. Totang05) Release 2 and pull hands apart (Illus. Totang06).*

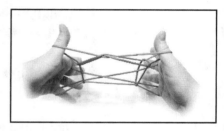

TOTANG05

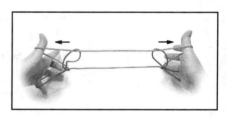

TOTANG06

He made the tent, dropped the strings,
and the little boys ran away.
He won!

"Well ... you are very good too," said the men.
"Why don't we play two out of three... for winners."

"All right."

The little boy was sure he could win.

"But don't forget it's *my* turn to name the figure we will make this time," said the man.

"That's fair."

The little boy got ready to begin the string figure.
He knew many string figures.
What would the man name ... ?

"The string figure we shall make ... ," said the man,
"is the string figure called ...
TOTANGUAK!"

The little boy shrank in horror.

He knew now he was playing with the string figure spirit himself ...
TOTANGUAK!

If he didn't win this game,
Totanguak would take him away forever.

And the string figure called Totanguak is so complicated
that it takes yards and yards of string to complete.

But the boy had to *try.*

He began weaving the first steps of the figure on his hands ...

> *Quickly begin making the tent figure again.*

Then he looked up.

Totanguak had already used all of the string on his hands and he had begun
to TAKE OUT HIS OWN INTESTINES ...

> *Demonstrate Totanguak pulling out his own intestines.*

and weave them into the figure ...
yard ... after yard ... after yard ...
until he held one great glistening mass

> *Pretend to hold the mass in your hands.*

woven into the string figure called
TOTANGUAK.

The little boy knew he had lost.
He knew he would be taken away forever.

But just then his father woke up and sat up in bed.
Totanguak vanished.
The little boy was saved.

Never again did he take out his string to play
when he should have been sleeping.

And let this be a lesson to you.
If you cannot sleep at night
don't get up and begin to play games.

Just turn over and go back to sleep,
lest you should look over in the corner of your room
and see ...
TOTANGUAK ...
waiting to play with *you*.

Notes: Margaret Read MacDonald says you should try to gross out your audience when you get to the part about Totanguak's intestines. She recommends that for younger audiences you may want to explain what intestines are before you begin.

The story of "Totanguak, Spirit of String Figures" is included in Field's *Eskimo Songs and Stories* (38-41). Helfman's book also discusses the spirit of the strings.

12. "The Tallow Dips," A Traditional Tale

Tallow dips refers to candles that are made by dipping a wick into hot wax many times until the candle is as thick as you want it. It may be helpful to show children some real tallow candles so they can see how they are hooked together.

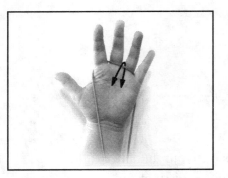

TALLOW01

1. *(Illus. Tallow01) Hang the string over L2 and L5. There is a palmar string passing in front of L3 and L4. R1 and R2 pick up this string and pull it out as far as it will go.*

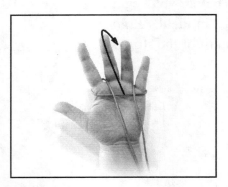

TALLOW02

2. *(Illus. Tallow02) With R1 and R2 pick up the new palmar string where it crosses in front of L3 and L4. Lift it over the back of the hand where it now crosses behind L3 and L4.*

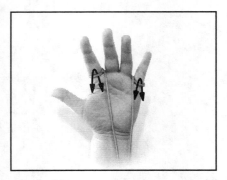

TALLOW03

3. *(Illus. Tallow03) R2 hooks down in the loop on L2 and R3 hooks down in the loop on L5. They pull out on these loops as far as they will go. A string now lays in front of L3 and L4.*

4. *(Illus. Tallow04) With R still holding the loops taut, L2 bends down over L2n, L3 bends down into the L2 loop, L4 bends down into the L5 loop, and L5 bends down over L5f.*

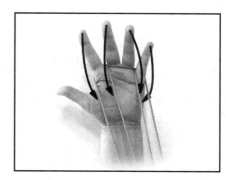

TALLOW04

5. *(Illus. Tallow05) Close L into a fist. There is now one string coming out between L2 and L3, two between L3 and L4 and one between L4 and L5. There is a loop around L2 and L5 and one around both L3 and L4. Lift the loop around L3 and L4 slightly. Insert the two loops held by R under this loop.*

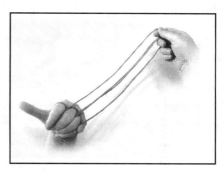

TALLOW05

6. *(Illus. Tallow06) Pull the loops back over L as far as they will go.*

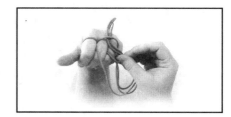

TALLOW06

7. *(Illus. Tallow07) Pull the loop that goes over L3 and L4 to the front of the hand. (Illus. Tallow08)*

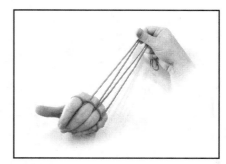

TALLOW07

TALLOW08

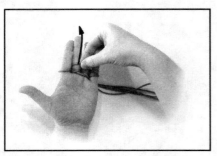

TALLOW09

8. *(Illus. Tallow09) Lift up and four loops will form—the tallow candles (Illus. Tallow10).*

A thief steals a bunch of tallow candles and takes them home with him.

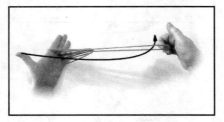

TALLOW10

TALLOW11

9. *Hang the loop from R onto L1 (Illus. Tallow11).*

He hangs them on a peg.

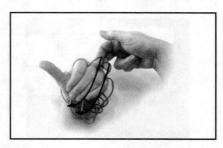

TALLOW12

10. *R2 picks up the loop on the back of L3 and R3 picks up the loop on the back of L4. (Illus. Tallow12) Hold L flat with palm up. This is the chair (Illus. Tallow13).*

He is tired so he sits down in a chair and falls asleep.

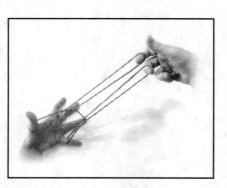

TALLOW13

When he awakens it is dark. He gets a pair of scissors to cut off one of the candles.

11. Release L1. This is the scissors (Illus. Tallow14).

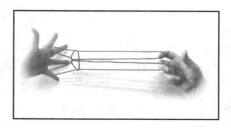

TALLOW14

Then he hears a knock at the door. He opens it to find a policeman standing there with his nightstick.

12. Release L2 and partially extend. This is the nightstick (Illus. Tallow15). (A shorter string than usual is shown.)

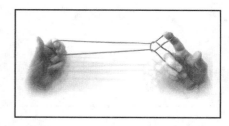

TALLOW15

The policeman puts him into handcuffs and arrests him for stealing the tallow candles. He is taken off to jail.

13. Release R2. Put L into loop held by L3 and R into loop held by R3. These are the handcuffs (Illus. Tallow16). (Normal string is shown again.)

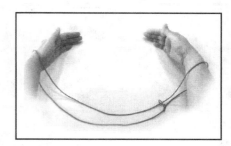

TALLOW16

Notes: This series of figures is unusual because it appears to originally have been known only in Europe and Hawaii, and nowhere else (Abraham 36). There are very many variations of the story to be found in print. You can locate some in DeWitt *String Figures II (22)*, Jayne (248), Johnson *String Games* (66), and Abraham (36). Abraham's version ends with "trial by jury results in acquittal" or "in hanging."

13. "Anansi the Spider" as told by Barbara G. Schutzgruber

Barbara G. Schutzgruber is a professional storyteller. You can see her perform Anansi and other string stories on her videotape *String Things: Stories, Games and Fun*. The videotape also shows how to make several figures. The videotape may be ordered from her Web site <http://www.bgsg-story.com/>.

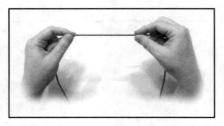

SPIDER01

1. *(Illus. Spider01) Hold the string in both hands so there is a straight segment between the hands.*

SPIDER02

2. *(Illus. Spider02) Twist this segment so a circle forms.*

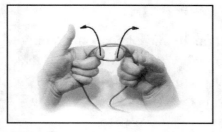

SPIDER03

3. *From behind, insert 2 into the circle. (Illus. Spider03) Release the string from all the other fingers. Extend and return to position. There will now be an upper and a lower loop on 2. Keep them separate.*

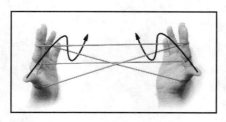

SPIDER04

4. *(Illus. Spider04) 1 goes over lower 2n only and picks up lower 2f.*

SPIDER05

5. *(Illus. Spider05) 1 goes over upper 2n and picks up upper 2f.*

6. (Illus. Spider06) 5 hooks down over upper 2n and pulls back.

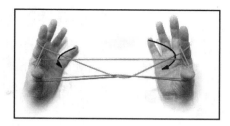

SPIDER06

7. (Illus. Spider07) 5 then picks up lower 2n. Return to position. The first string drops off 5.

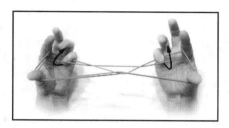

SPIDER07

8. (Illus. Spider08) A triangle forms in the 5 loops. 2 goes into the 5 loops from above and picks up the base of the triangle and returns to position.

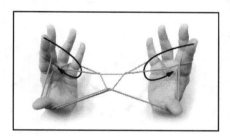

SPIDER08

9. (Illus. Spider09) 1 releases their loops. A letter W forms in the middle of the figure.

SPIDER09

10. (Illus. Spider10) 1 goes into the 5 loop from below and brings back on its back the two side strings of the W. R1 brings back the two strings on the right of the W and L1 the two strings on the left.

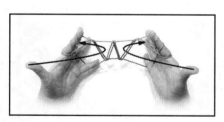

SPIDER10

11. (Illus. Spider11) Remove all the loops from 2. You may need to use the opposite hand to help slide all the loops off 2.

SPIDER11

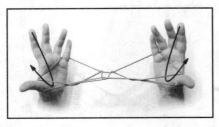

SPIDER12

12. *(Illus. Spider12) 2 goes from below into the 1 loops and picks up the 1f strings.*

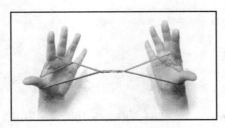

SPIDER13

13. *(Illus. Spider13) Release the 1 loops.*

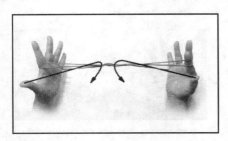

SPIDER14

14. *(Illus. Spider14) 1 goes under all the loops and brings back the 5f strings. Return to position.*

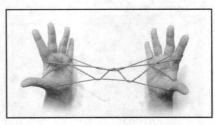

SPIDER15

15. *(Illus. Spider15) Release 5 loops.*

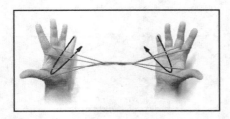

SPIDER16

16. *(Illus. Spider16) 5 goes under 2 loops into 1 loop from below. 5 brings back the 1f string.*

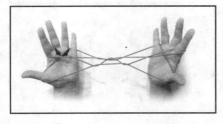

SPIDER17

17. *(Illus. Spider17) R1 and R2 go into the L2 loop from above and picks up the L palmar string and pulls it through the L2 loops.*

18. *(Illus. Spider18) While R1 and R2 hold the L palmar string, L1 and L5 release their loops. (Illus. Spider19) Put the palmar string back on L1 and L5 so that it now runs over the L2 loop (Illus. Spider20).*

SPIDER18

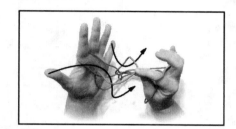

SPIDER19

SPIDER20

19. *R1 and R2 remove L2 loop (Illus. Spider21) and place it over the back of L (Illus. Spider22).*

SPIDER21

SPIDER22

SPIDER23

20. Repeat Steps 17 through 19 on R (Illus. Spider23).

SPIDER24

21. R1 and R2 grab L1f and L5n (Illus. Spider24). They hold onto them while L slips out of all its loops (Illus. Spider25). Put L1 and L5 back into their loops that were being held by R (Illus. Spider26).

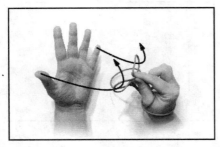

SPIDER25

SPIDER26

22. Repeat Step 21 on R.

SPIDER27

23. (Illus. Spider27) R2 goes from below into R1 loop and removes it.

24. *(Illus. Spider28) R1 removes L1 loop from below.*

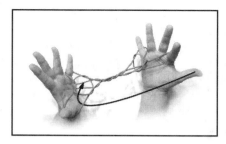

SPIDER28

25. *(Illus. Spider29) L1 removes L5 loop from below.*

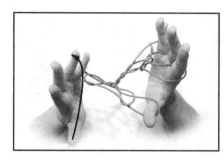

SPIDER29

26. *(Illus. Spider30) L5 removes R5 loop from below.*

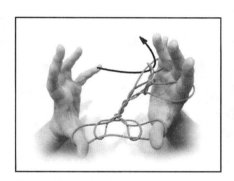

SPIDER30

27. *(Illus. Spider31) R5 removes R2 loop from below. Extend.*

SPIDER31

28. *(Illus. Spider32) 1 enters 5 loops from above and removes 5.*

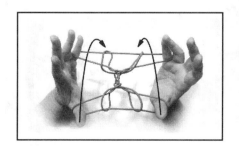

SPIDER32

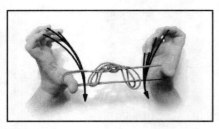

SPIDER33

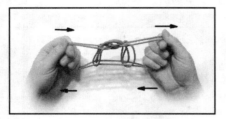

SPIDER34

29. *(Illus. Spider33) 2, 3, 4, and 5 enter 1 loops from below. 1 comes out of loops.*

30. *(Illus. Spider34) This is Anansi. Tip the hands from side to side and the spider will run from one hand to the other.*

The people of West Africa tell stories of a character named Anansi, the spider-man. In those stories, sometimes Anansi looks like a spider. Sometimes he looks like a man. Sometimes he looks like a man with spider legs. And sometimes he looks like a spider with a man's head. But no matter what Anansi looks like ... he loves parties. He is the original "party guy." He has a wonderful time at parties. He loves to dance at parties. He loves to eat at parties. Anansi has a very large waist. But when it's time to clean up, Anansi is as far away as possible.

Begin the figure through Step 9.

One day, Anansi heard that there would be two parties happening on opposite sides of the hills.

Display the W as in Step 10.

Wanting to know what was going on at those parties, he walked over to the first village

Walk to the one side of the stage. Continue making the figure but don't draw attention to it.

and said, "Hey guys ... I hear you're having a party." They said, "Yes, Anansi. Are you going to stay?" He said, "What are you going to eat?" They said, "We've got some beans cooking." Anansi said, "Mmmm ... I love beans. Are you done yet?" And everybody said, "Well no, not yet. Are you going to stay anyway?" Anansi said, "Well ... I'll be back."

Walk to the other side of the stage.

Well he walked …
and walked …
and walked.
Finally he got to the second village and he said, "Hey guys… I hear you're having a party!"
They all said, "Yeah, Anansi. Are you going to stay?"
He said, "What are you going to eat?"
They said, "Well, we've got some yams cooking and some sweet potatoes."
Anansi said, "Mmmm … Mmm … I love yams. Are they done yet?"
They all said, "No, not yet. Are you going to stay?"
And Anansi said, "I'll be back."

Walk back to the center of the stage.

Well, Anansi wanted to be at both parties so he could eat at both parties. But how would he know when the beans and the yams would be ready? This was before the days of cell phones and pagers. Anansi had a brilliant idea! He tied a rope around his very large waist. He sent one son to the first village with one end of the rope, and another son to the second village with the other end of the rope.

Display Anansi.

"When the food is ready, pull on the rope and I'll know it's time to eat."

Pull Anansi from one side to the other.

Anansi sat between those two villages …

Put Anansi in the middle

and he waited.
And guess what happened? They ate at the same time. He got a little tug from one side.

Pull Anansi to one side.

Yes! It's the beans! Then he got a little tug from the other side.

Pull Anansi to the other side.

No … wait a minute … it's the yams!

Continue pulling from one side to the other.

Nope, it's the beans over here.
No, wait, it's the yams over there.
Beans.
Yams.
Beans.
Yams.
And he was pulled back and forth ...
and back and forth ...
and he wasn't getting anyplace.

Stop pulling. Put fists together to take attention away from the
figure.

Now, at the two villages, they were getting worried. It was not like Anansi
to miss a party. At the first village, they talked it over and decided that the
rope must be stuck. They got six of the biggest guys to pull on the rope.
And at the other village, same idea! So they got six of the biggest guys to
pull on the rope. They pulled him one way and they pulled him another.

Pull emphatically one way and then the other. Continue
pulling back and forth.

Anansi jerked back and forth ...
and back and forth ...
and back and forth.
And the rope got tighter ...
and tighter ...
and tighter ...
and tighter ...
until Anansi had a very small waist!

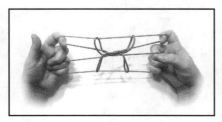

There are two loops around 2, 3, 4, and 5. 1 moves in
between the two loops where it is being held by the
other fingers and removes the front loop. Remove 2
from the other loop. 2 enters 1 loop from above and
removes it from 1. Extend (Illus. Spider35).

SPIDER35

Anansi looked down at the tiny, little waist and thought, "Yuck! Who wants
a skinny, little waist?" He was so upset that he ran off

Display Anansi again as in Step 30.

and hid in the tall grass.

Gather string into the fist of one hand.

To this day, if you go out into the fields, you can still find spiders curled up and hiding in the tall grass.

Point to your fingers curled around the string.

And the next time you see a spider, look at it very carefully. Because if that spider has a teeny, tiny, skinny, little waist, then you know that THAT spider IS one of Anansi's many, many children.

Notes: The figure that Barbara uses to portray Anansi is The Porker or The Pig (Gryski, *Super* 70). Abraham indicates that it was collected by R. H. Compton in 1919 on the South Sea Islands of Lifou and Uvea (82).

Barbara shared how she became interested in string figures: "In the late 1970's I attended the concert of a folk singer. What is etched in my memory 25 years later, is not her name, or her music but that she demonstrated a string figure she had learned while on tour in Australia. It was a dog that moved back and forth. I was fascinated. The only string game I remember playing as a child is Cat's Cradle … and I always got stuck in that endless loop repeating the first few steps over and over, never finding a way out. But this … now this was COOL! I wanted to learn more but had no idea of where to look. Eventually I came across *The Story Vine* by Anne Pelowski. Here were individual string figures used with stories *and* a bibliography of resources. I was on my way. I read as much as I could about how string figures are used within different cultures around the world but found few stories connected to individual figures. In 1987 I attended the Toronto Storytelling Festival where Camilla Gryski was on the program. Camilla's hands were magical as she made stars appear and multiply, bears run away from caves, monkeys climb trees and not only used a single figure in a story but incorporated multiple figures in a single story. I was inspired … the possibilities were endless. On the train trip back to Detroit I played with the figures I knew and created my first original string story. Since then I am continually learning new figures—what different things do they look like, how do they move and flow. As a storyteller, I use them to illustrate folktales, fables and nursery rhymes and I also write new stories to go along with them."

14. "The Two Old Women" as told by David Titus

This story was shared by storyteller Dave Titus. He learned the first part from Rita Bloominstein, a native woman who lives in Palmar, Alaska but was born on Nelson Island.

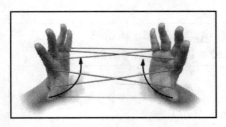

LADIES01

1. *Opening A (Illus. Ladies01). From below, 1 removes 2 loop.*

I have a friend in Alaska and she told me this story.

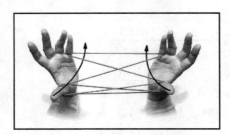

LADIES02

2. *(Illus. Ladies02) From below, 1 removes 5 loop. There are now three loops on 1.*

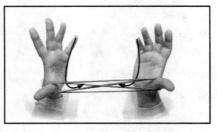

LADIES03

3. *(Illus. Ladies03) From below, 5 enters 1 loop, L5 on the left of the X that crosses in the middle, R5 on the right of the X.*

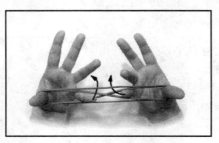

LADIES04

4. *(Illus. Ladies 04) L5 and R5 push down on X until they pass under 1f transverse (passing straight from L1 and R1).*

5. *(Illus. Ladies05) 5 hooks down 1f transverse (Illus. Ladies06). The other loops slide off 5.*

LADIES05

LADIES06

6. *(Illus. Ladies 07) 2 and 3 enter 1 from above.*

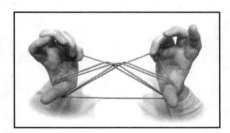

LADIES07

When I get up in the morning I should look like this.

7. *(Illus. Ladies08) Pinch transverse 1n between 2 and 3 (Illus. Ladies09) and return to position while catching it on the back of 2. Release 1 loops.*

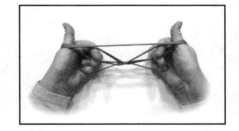

LADIES08

LADIES09

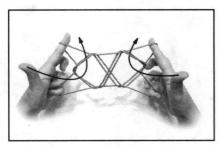

Ladies10

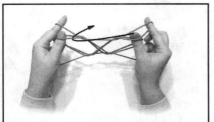
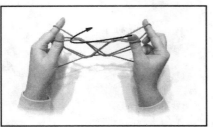

Ladies11

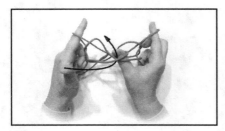

Ladies12

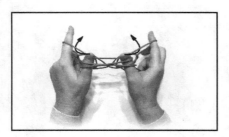

Ladies13

8. *(Illus. Ladies10) There is one string in the middle X that comes across the front of the X. R1 picks it up from underneath where it is closest to R2. On the left side there is one string that goes down and becomes the L5 loop. The other string is the one you want to pick up with L1 from underneath close to L2.*

9. *(Illus. Ladies 11) R1 removes L1 loop from below.*

10. *(Illus. Ladies12) L1 enters both loops on R1 from below. L1 and R1 extend.*

11. *(Illus. Ladies13) 1 enters 2 loop from below.*

But before I have had my coffee, I look like this.

12. (Illus. Ladies14) L1 and R1 pull the 2n string back through the 1 loops and the loop slips off 2. The other two strings slip off 1. Do not extend. Allow the loops that came off 1 to hang loosely. You might need to pull these loops down with 2 and 3 so they look like bags under someone's eyes (Illus. Ladies15) (Illus. Ladies16).

LADIES14

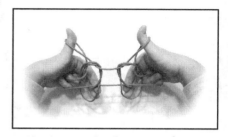

LADIES15

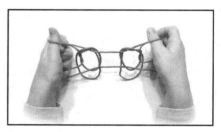

LADIES16

After I have had my coffee, I put on my glasses and look like this

13. 2 enters 1 loop from underneath and removes from 1 (Illus. Ladies17). 1 enters the "eyes" and pull to the middle while 2 extends so the "bags" disappear (Illus. Ladies18).

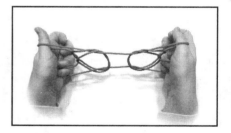

LADIES17

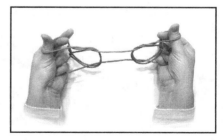

LADIES18

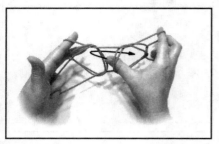

LADIES19

14. *(Illus. Ladies19) R1 enters the right "eye" and pushes the two right strings in the middle of the figure over the two left strings in the middle. R1 grabs the two left strings.*

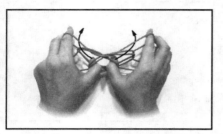

LADIES20

15. *(Illus. Ladies20) L1 enters the loops next to R1 and picks up the other two strings. R1 and L1 pull back, each catching two strings on the back of 1. 1 enters 2 from below.*

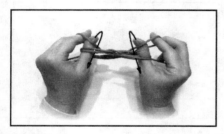

LADIES21

16. *(Illus. Ladies21) 1 hooks 2n and pulls it back through the two loops on 1. The loop slips off 2 and the other two loops slip off 1. 2 enters the 1 loop from above and removes it. Extend, spreading 2 and 5 as far apart as you can. Bring the hands together and extend twice, repeating to simulate a beating heart (Illus. Ladies22).*

and my heart starts beating.

LADIES22

17. *There are two strings that pass in front of the 1 loops on each side of the bottom of the heart. R1 picks up the two strings closest to it, L1 does the same on the other side.*

18. *(Illus. Ladies23) L1 enters the R1 loops from below and removes the loops from R1.*

LADIES23

19. *(Illus. Ladies24) R1 enters all the loops on L1 from below.*

LADIES24

20. *(Illus. Ladies25) 1 enters 2 loop from above catching 2f and bringing it back through the 1 loops.*

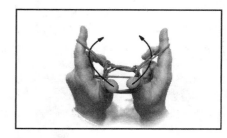

LADIES25

Then my friend told me a story of two old women. Two old women were trapping animals to get skins for parkas for their grand-children. They divided up the skins and had one extra.

21. *(Illus. Ladies26) The loop slips off 2 and the other loops slip off 1. Insert 2 into 1 from below and remove from 1. Extend carefully just until two "ladies" appear (Illus. Ladies27).*

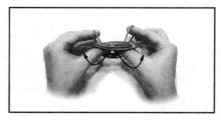

LADIES26

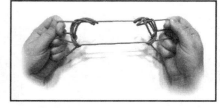

LADIES27

"I should have it. My granddaughter is taller."

22. *Tip right hand toward left hand so right lady appears to be talking.*

"No, my grandson is bigger."

23. *Tip left hand toward right hand so left lady appears to be talking.*

The two old women got in a fight and pulled each other's hair out.

24. *Alternate tipping. Bring both hands together so women appear to be fighting.*

Suddenly the two old women stopped.

25. *Hold figure still.*

They look down at the hair on the ground.

26. *Tip both hands so the figures tip to the middle.*

They looked at each other. They were BALD! They couldn't go back into their village looking like that. They threw the hair up into the trees so no one could see it

and they flew up into the trees and became eagles. BALD EAGLES!

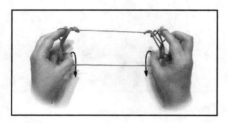

LADIES28

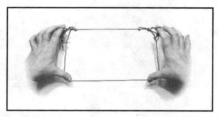

LADIES29

27. *Insert 3 next to 2. Remove 2. Insert 2 into the opposite side of the loop as before. Remove 3. 1 presses down on the string that goes across the bottom of the figure (Illus. Ladies28). Remove 5 and extend. As you extend, the women disappear and "birds" move up toward 2 (Illus. Ladies29).*

Notes: The story of the two old women is a very old one. Different versions have the women turning into ptarmigan or flying squirrels. Titus turned them into eagles because he loved the humor of "bald" eagles. The natives, of course, did not call them bald eagles, (actually they are Balde from the Old English for white) but had another name for them.

15. "The Park" by Crystal Brown

Storyteller Crystal Brown likes to write a new story that incorporates string figures every year to share with children.

Once upon a time there was a girl. It was her birthday, and for her birthday she received a beautiful necklace.

1. Double the string and put it around your neck. From underneath, put L1 into the loop and put the two strings on L1. Put one string near the bottom of L1 and one string near the top. L1 is facing up.

2. (Illus. Necklace01) Turn L clockwise so that L1 is now facing down.

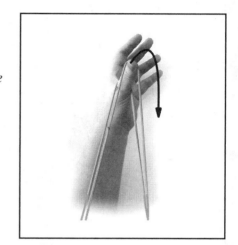

NECKLACE01

3. (Illus. Necklace02) R reaches over the strings and R1 takes the loop off L1 that is near the tip.

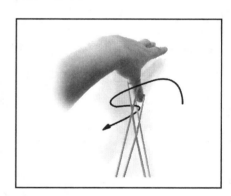

NECKLACE02

4. (Illus. Necklace03) Carry this loop back over the strings, turning it over as you go. At the same time, turn L1 so it is facing up again.

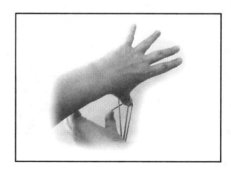

NECKLACE03

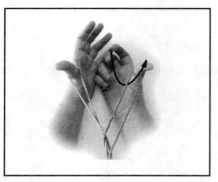

NECKLACE04

5. *(Illus. Necklace04) Put the loop onto L5.*

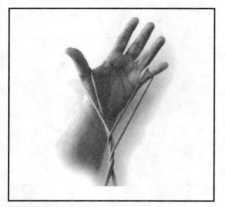

NECKLACE05

6. *(Illus. Necklace05) R1 and R2 reach through the loop on L5 and grab L1f (Illus. Necklace06).*

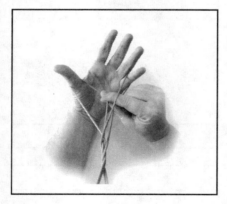

NECKLACE06

When she put it on and looked in the mirror she thought she looked gorgeous. She looked so wonderful she wanted everyone to see her wearing this beautiful necklace.

She decided to walk through the town to show off her necklace. Soon, she came to the city park. She thought this would be the perfect place to go because everyone went to the park and they would see her in her necklace. So she opened up the gate and went in.

7. *(Illus. Necklace07) Release L5 (Illus. Necklace08).*[A]

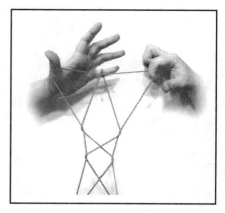

NECKLACE07

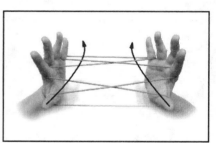

NECKLACE08

1. *(Illus. Gate01) Opening A. 1 picks up 5n.*

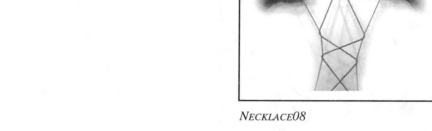

GATE01

2. *(Illus. Gate02) 5 picks up 1f.*

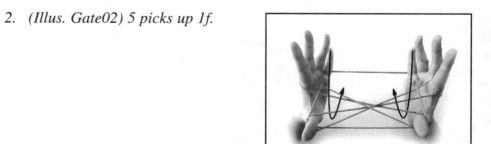

GATE02

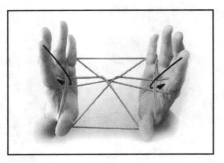

3. *(Illus. Gate03) 2 bends over dou-ble palmar string and holds to palm of hand.*

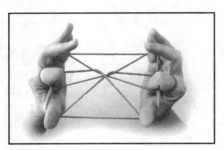

4. *(Illus. Gate04) 5 and 1 release their loops. Let the old loop drop off 2. Do NOT pull taut yet. 3, 4, and 5 enter the 2 loops.*

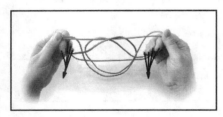

5. *(Illus. Gate05) 2 lifts up.*

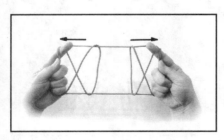

6. *(Illus. Gate06) Pull your hands apart and let the strings slide between your fingers. The gate comes open.[B]*

She walked down the path until she came to a park bench. She decided to sit down where everyone could see her. As soon as she sat down she began to notice what was in the park. The first thing she saw were the beautiful flowers.

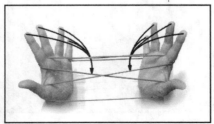

1. *(Illus. Laia01) Opening A. 2, 3, 4, and 5 tip down into the 5 loop.*

2. *(Illus. Laia02) Throw the loop back over these fingers, making sure that 1 does not go into this loop. 5 will no longer have a loop. There is now a loop around 2, 3, and 4. Put it toward the tops of these fingers.*

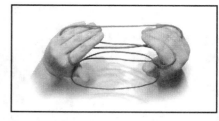

LAIA02

2. *(Illus. Laia03) Put 1 and 5 into this loop and let it drop down around your wrists.*

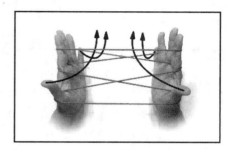

LAIA03

3. *(Illus. Laia04) R5 goes under all the strings, including the front transverse wrist string. R5 hooks down on the 1n string. R5 returns to position, carrying the 1n string on its back.*

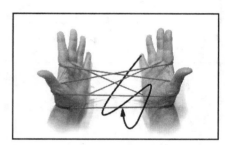

LAIA04

5. *(Illus. Laia05) L5 enters the R5 loop from below and shares the loop. Hands return to position.*

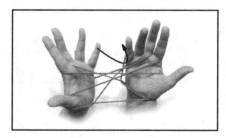

LAIA05

6. *(Illus. Laia06) 1 enters 2 loop from below. Remove 2, transferring loop to 1.*

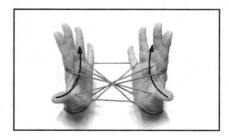

LAIA06

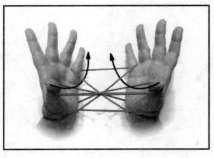

LAIA07

7. *(Illus. Laia07) 1 picks up 5n.*

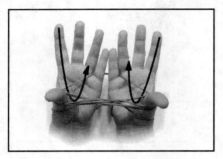

LAIA08

8. *(Illus. Laia08) 2 enters 1 loop from below and picks up double 1f.*

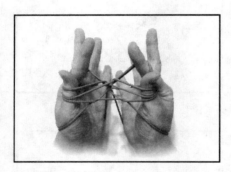

LAIA09

9. *(Illus. Laia09) Release 5 loops.*

LAIA10

10. *(Illus. Laia10) 5 picks up lower 2f loop and returns.*

11. *(Illus. Laia11) 1 releases all its loops.*

LAIA11

12. *(Illus. Laia12) Turn your hands so 2, 3, 4, and 5 point away from you and 1 points up.^{C}*

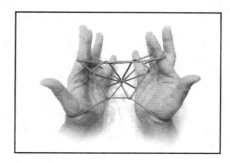

LAIA12

As soon as she noticed the flowers she saw what was fluttering over them.

1. *Put 1 into loop. Put L5 into loop as in Position 1. (String shown is shorter than usual.)*

2. *(Illus. JButterfly01) R5 goes down behind the L palmar string. Turn R5 away from you and up. Return to position.*

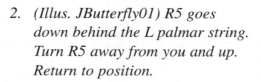

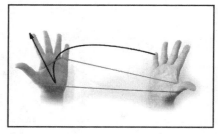

JBUTTERFLY01

3. *(Illus. JButterfly03) (Normal string is shown.) 2 picks up 5n.*

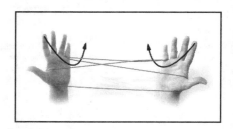

JBUTTERFLY03

4. *(Illus. JButterfly04) Do the Opening A move with 3, picking up the strings that cross in front of 3 and 4. R3 picks up its string from L first, then L3 picks up its string from R.*

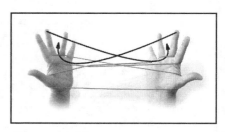

JBUTTERFLY04

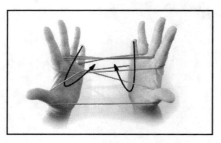

JBUTTERFLY05

5. *(Illus. JButterfly05) Turn the fingers so they face you. 5 goes over all the strings to pick up 1f. Return to position.*

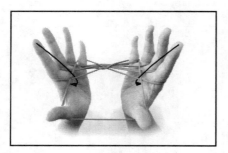

JBUTTERFLY06

6. *(Illus. JButterfly06) 2 hooks down over the palmar string where it passes in front and holds it to the palm.*

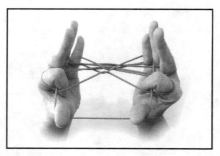

JBUTTERFLY07

7. *(Illus. JButterfly07) 1 releases its loop. With 2 still hooking down on the palmar string, turn the palms toward you so the old 2 loops slide off. Straighten up 2. The strings that were hooked down before become the new 2 loops. Point your fingers away from you to show off the butterfly (Illus. JButterfly08).*[D]

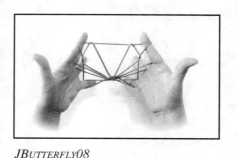

JBUTTERFLY08

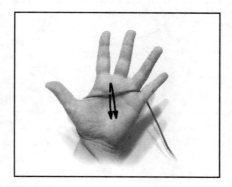

BIRD01

1. *Hang the string on L1 and L5. (Illus. Bird01) R2 hooks down on the L palmar string and pulls it down as far as it will go.*

Then she heard "tweet, tweet." It was a bird,

2. *(Illus. Bird02) R2 hooks down on the new L palmar string and again pulls it down as far as it will go.*

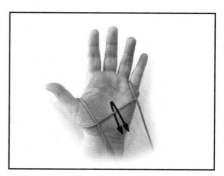

BIRD02

3. *(Illus. Bird03) R enters the loop hanging from L from above. R1 and R5 lift up so the strings of the hanging loop rest on them.*

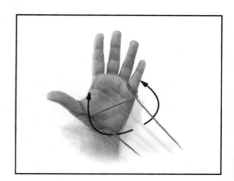

BIRD03

5. *(Illus. Bird04) R1 enters the L1 loop from above. R5 enters the L5 loop from above. R1 and R5 fingertips touch.*

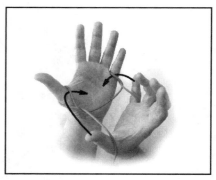

BIRD04

6. *(Illus. Bird05) R1 and R5 pull back so the L hanging loop slips off them. Fully extend. Hold L straight up. R1 and R5 release their loops which now hang in front of L.*

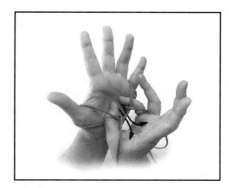

BIRD05

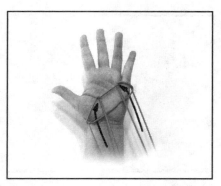

Bird06

7. *(Illus. Bird06) R1 picks up the bottom string of the triangle in the L1 loop. R5 picks up the bottom string of the triangle in the L5 loop. Extend.*

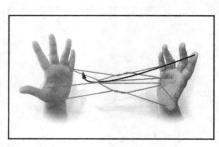

Bird07

8. *(Illus. Bird07) There is one string that is the L1f and turns into the L5n string. R2 picks up that string from the middle of the figure.*

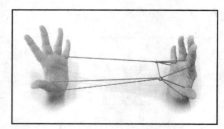

Bird08

9. *(Illus. Bird08) Turn R from side to side to tighten knots that will form in front of R1 and R5. Release R1 and R5 (Illus. Bird09).*

10. *Pull hands apart and loops will move from R to L.*[E]

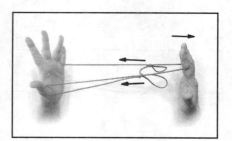

Bird09

but the bird was hidden among the leaves. She couldn't see him, but listened to his song until she spotted him but as soon as she saw him he flew away.

Now she had been sitting there so quietly for so long that another little creature hopped out to look at her. It was a rabbit.

1. *Opening A (Illus. Rabbit01). From underneath, 2 removes the 1 loop. Keep this loop near the fingertips of 2.*

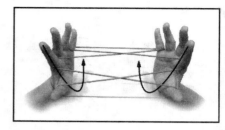

RABBIT01

2. *(Illus. Rabbit02) Turn your hands away from you. There are now two transverse strings, the 5f and the upper 2n strings. In between are four crossed strings. 1 goes into the 5 loop from below and brings back the four crossed strings on the back of 1.*

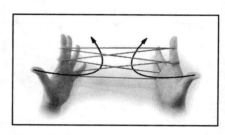

RABBIT02

3. *(Illus. Rabbit03) 1 hooks down on the upper 2n string. The four strings on 1 slide off.*

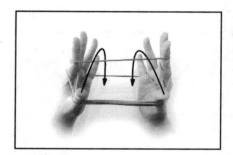

RABBIT03

4. *(Illus. Rabbit04) Still hooking down that string, 1 goes under the other strings and picks up 5f.*

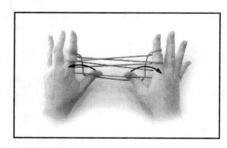

RABBIT04

5. *(Illus. Rabbit05) From underneath, 1 goes into upper 2 loop. These are the loops that are twisted.*

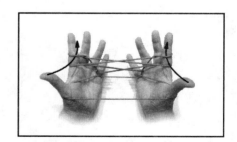

RABBIT05

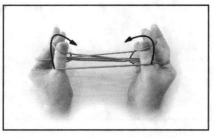

RABBIT06

6. *(Illus. Rabbit06) Navajo the thumb loops.*

RABBIT07

7. *(Illus. Rabbit07) Take 2 out of the upper loops.*

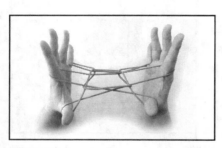

RABBIT08

8. *(Illus. Rabbit08) 5 releases its loops. Do not pull taut.*

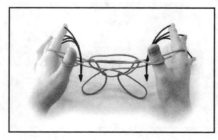

RABBIT09

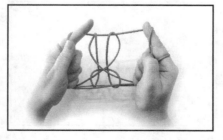

RABBIT10

9. *(Illus. Rabbit09) 2, 3, 4, and 5 go down into the 1 loop. 2 goes under the 1n string and then straightens up, carrying the string on its back. 1 slides out of its loop. Pull the hands apart. The rabbit's ears will pop up. You may need to use your thumbs to arrange the strings (Illus. Rabbit10).*[F]

Suddenly she noticed the sun was beginning to go down. She had forgotten the time. She thought, "I'd better go home or my mother will be worried." So she started home just as the first star appeared in the sky.

1.   Opening A. (Illus. StarMoon01) Release 1 loops. Pull taut.

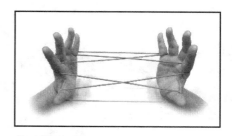

StarMoon01

2.   (Illus. StarMoon02) R1 holds down strings of R2 loop and R5n. R2 hooks down over R5f string and pulls it back as it straightens up (Illus. StarmMoon03).

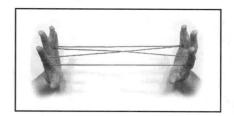

StarMoon02

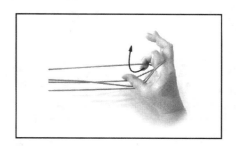

StarMoon03

3.   (Illus. StarMoon04) L2 enters the top R2 loop from below and shares it.

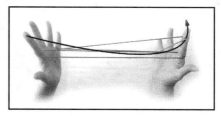

StarMoon04

4.   (Illus. StarMoon05) 1 goes under the 2 loops and picks up 5n and returns.

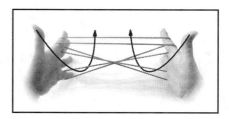

StarMoon05

5.   (Illus. StarMoon06) 1 goes up into upper 2 loops and shares them.

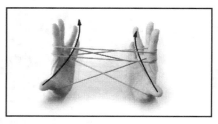

StarMoon06

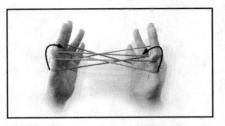

StarMoon07

6. *(Illus. StarMoon07) Navajo the 1 loop.*

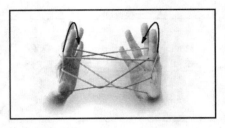

StarMoon08

7. *(Illus. StarMoon08) Let the upper loop on 2 slip off. There should still be a lower loop on 2. This is the star (Illus. StarMoon09).*

She reached home just as the moon sailed overhead.

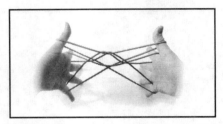

StarMoon09

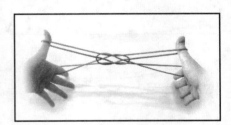

StarMoon10

8. *Now release the 5 loop and pull hands gently apart (Illus. StarMoon10). Raise your hands over your head.*[G]

Her mother was waiting on the porch. The girl said, "Mother, I love my beautiful necklace but it is not as beautiful as all the things I saw today in the park."

Notes:

[A]The figure that Crystal Brown uses for a necklace is called The Camp Bed by Gryski (*Many Stars* 16). [B]This figure is called Open the Gate in Hawaii. (Gryski, *Many Stars* 22).

The Laia Flower or Lotus Flower comes from the New [C]Hebrides (Gryski, *Many Stars* 44). Abraham instead calls it The Laia Fruit (54).

[D]This is the Japanese Butterfly (Gryski, *Many Stars* 24).

[E]Johnson calls this Flying Bird and tells that it comes from New Guinea (*String Games* 49).

[F]Rabbit is a Klamath Indian figure (Jayne 79).

[G]The figure that Brown uses to represent the star and moon is known as The Giant Clam from Fiji (Gryski, *Many Stars* 28).

16. "The Leprechaun" by Crystal Brown

Once upon a time there was a little leprechaun. He was singing and dancing, singing and dancing because he had found a bag of gold, and now he was rich.

1. *(Illus. Hoochie01) Begin with Position 1 with a twist in the string to form an X in the middle. (String is shorter than normal.) Opening A.*

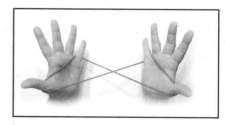

HOOCHIE01

2. *(Illus. Hoochie02) 1 goes under the 2 loop and picks up 5n and brings it back. (Normal string is shown.)*

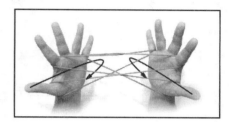

HOOCHIE02

3. *(Illus. Hoochie03) 5 hooks down 2f and picks up 1f. 5 returns through the 2 loops.*

HOOCHIE03

He was singing so loudly he didn't know a witch heard him. She crept out of the forest and peeked in the window. She saw the bag of gold sitting on the table. While he was singing and dancing she quietly opened the window, stole his bag of gold and took it to her den in the forest.

4. *(Illus. Hoochie04) Release 2 loops.*

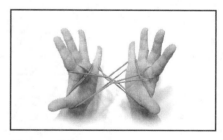

HOOCHIE04

5. *(Illus. Hoochie05) Make the figure dance by bringing 5 together and then 1 together.[A]*

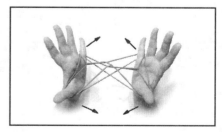

HOOCHIE05

Keep previous figure going—then drop figure and mime opening window, snatching bag of gold.

Do the figure in "Totanguak" as found on page 46.[B]

Pretty soon the little leprechaun stopped dancing. He said, "Now I'm going to count the coins in my bag!" When he went to get it, it wasn't there. He looked all over his house but it was gone.

He thought someone must have stolen the bag but he didn't know who. He decided to think about what to do, and went into the kitchen and made himself a cup of tea.

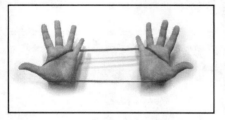

CUP01

1. *Double your string. Position 1 (Illus. Cup01) Opening A.*

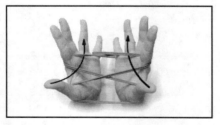

CUP02

2. *(Illus. Cup02) 1 picks up 2f.*

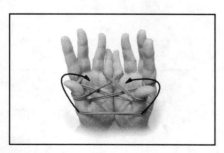

CUP03

3. *(Illus. Cup03) Navajo the loops on 1.*

4. (Illus. Cup04) Release 5. Pull figure taut. Hold figure with 1 on top to show cup and saucer. (Illus. Cup05)

Cup04

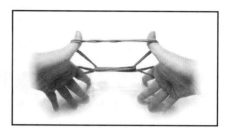

Cup05

Just as he was sipping his tea he heard a noise outside his window, "Who, whooo!" He saw up in the tree an owl.

5. Return to position. (Illus. Cup055) 1 picks up 2n.

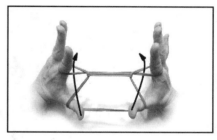

Cup055

6. (Illus. Cup06) Navajo the loops on 1.

Cup06

7. (Illus. Cup07) 2 hooks down on the string that crosses the middle of the figure.

Cup07

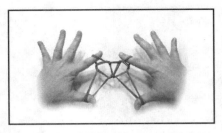

CUP08

8. *Turn your hands away from you. As you do this, the 2 loops will slip off 2 (Illus. Cup08).*[C]

Move owl's eyes up and away from your face.

Move owl's eyes to your face.

Move figure up and away.

Figure at your face.

"Oh, Mr. Owl," said the leprechaun, "did you see who stole my bag of gold?"

"Who, whooo, I saw a witch run through the forest. She was carrying a bag."

"Do you know where the witch's den is?" asked the leprechaun.

"No, you'll have to find it yourself."

So the little leprechaun decided to go into the forest by himself and look for the witch's den.

Now, if you know anything about witches' dens you know they're always guarded by a magic, secret door. If you can't find the magic secret door, you'll never find the witch's den.

The little leprechaun looked everywhere in the forest and finally he found a place between two trees covered with ivy and vines.

1. *Position 1 (String is shorter than normal.) (Illus. ADoor01) Put all of R hand under L palmar string. String will rest on back of R wrist.*

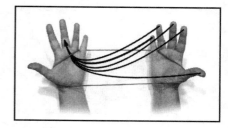

ADoor01

2. *(Illus. ADoor02) (Normal string is shown.) Put all of L hand under R palmar string. String will rest on back of L wrist.*

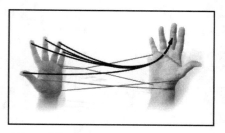

ADoor02

3. *(Illus. ADoor03) 1 picks up 5n.*

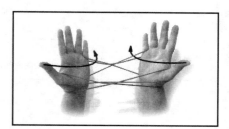

ADoor03

4. *(Illus. ADoor04) 5 picks up 1f.*

ADoor04

5. *(Illus. ADoor05) R grasps all strings in middle of figure.*

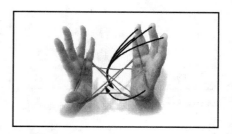

ADoor05

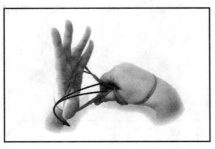

ADOOR06

6. (Illus. ADoor06) Lift them over L1 into the space between L1 and L2.

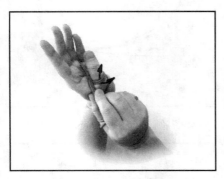

ADOOR07

7. (Illus. ADoor07) R lets go of those strings it is holding. R1 and R2 pinch the two strings that are wrapped around L1.

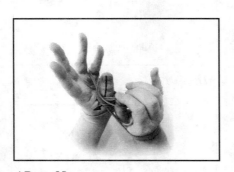

ADOOR08

8. (Illus. ADoor08) They continue to hold onto those strings as you remove L1 from all the strings that are wrapped around it.

ADOOR09

9. (Illus. ADoor09) From below, slide L1 back into the loops held by R1 and R2.

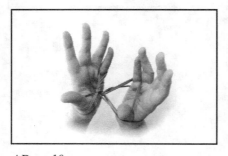

ADOOR10

10. (Illus. ADoor10) Repeat Steps 5 through 9 on R side.

11. (Illus. ADoor11) R1 and R2 pick up the string on the back of L and move it over all the fingers to the middle of the figure.

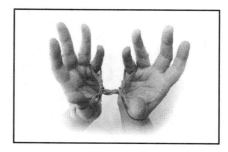

ADoor11

"Ivy, Ivy,
Ivy Green,
Let the witch's
door be seen."

And suddenly there appeared the magic secret door.

12. (Illus. ADoor12) L1 and L2 do the same to the string on the back of R.

13. Rub strings together.

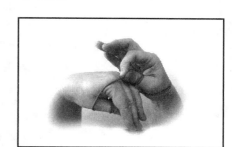

ADoor12

14. (Illus. ADoor13) Extend figure vertically.[D]

ADoor13

The leprechaun went into the den. He was lucky the witch was not in her den. He looked in all the rooms and finally he saw the bag of gold sitting on a table.

1. (Illus. Bag01) Hang the string on L1 and L5. Lift the L palmar string so it goes behind L3.

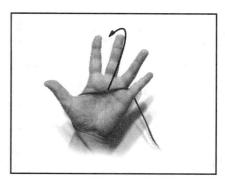

Bag01

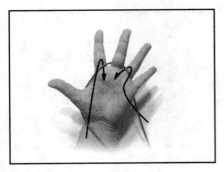

BAG02

2. *(Illus. Bag02) R goes under hanging loop. R2 hooks down on the string in front of L2. R3 hooks down on the string in front of L4 (Illus. Bag03). They pull out until the hanging loop comes up in front of L.*

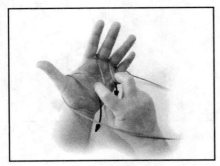

BAG03

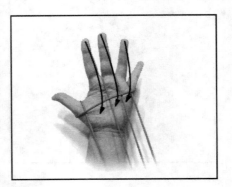

BAG04

3. *(Illus. Bag04) L2 bends down into the loop held by R2. L3 bends down into the space between the loops. L4 bends down into the loop held by R3.*

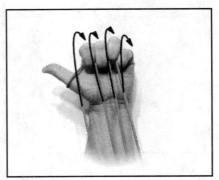

BAG05

4. *(Illus. Bag05) Lift the strings held by R2 and R3 over the back of L and let hang.*

5. *(Illus. Bag06) R2 hooks down on the string in front of L1. R3 hooks down on the string on front of L5.*

He snatched it up, ran home, and never let that witch steal it again.

6. *(Illus. Bag07) Hold L hand with palm up, fingers pointing away from you. R pulls up on those strings and pinches them together (Illus. Bag08).*[E]

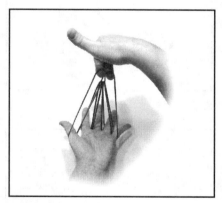

BAG06

BAG07

BAG08

Notes:

[A]Hoochie Koochie Man is a variation of Man on a Bed (Gryski, *Cat's Cradle* 57).

[B]Siberian House is from the Inuit (Gryski, *Cat's Cradle* 30).

[C]Most of us know the beginning of this figure as a Cup and Saucer. Leeming indicates that it is an outrigger canoe and comes from New Caledonia. It "represents a native canoe with an outrigger attached to one side. An outrigger is a long piece of wood fastened to the canoe by two beams. Its purpose is to keep the canoe from capsizing" (140). It is displayed "upside down" from the Cup and Saucer. Gryski adds that it's called a House in Japan when it's upside down and a Saki Cup when right side up (*Cat's Cradle*, 18). Gryski shows how to continue into the Owl's Eyes figure (*Cat's Cradle* 20).

[D]Apache Door is the first figure in Jayne's book. It was collected from an Apache girl from New Mexico (12). Abraham gives Mexican Hurdle as another name (68).

[E]This is the figure called The Parachute from Scotland (Gryski, *Cat's Cradle* 26).

17. "The Mother and the Ogre" by Crystal Brown

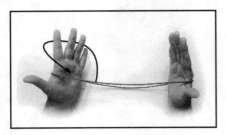

CRADLE01

1. *Put the string so it hangs on the backs of the fingers but not 1. (String shown is shorter than normal.) (Illus. Cradle01) R1 and R2 pick up the near string of the L hand loop and wraps it around the fingers on L.*

Once upon a time there was a boy. He didn't sleep in a bed. He slept in a hammock because that gently rocking hammock always put him right to sleep.

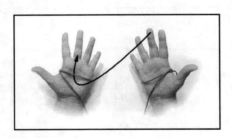

CRADLE02

2. *(Illus. Cradle02) L1 and L2 pick up the near string of the R hand loop and wraps it around the fingers on R.*

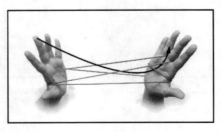

CRADLE03

3. *(Illus. Cradle03) (Normal string is shown.) R3 picks up L palmar string.*

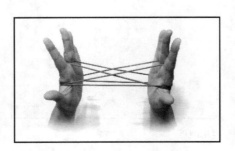

CRADLE04

4. *(Illus. Cradle04) Between the loop on R3, L3 picks up the R palmar string and extends.[A]*

5. *(Illus. Cradle05) Rock the figure.*

6. *Do Steps 1 though 5 of the figure in "Totanguak" found on page 46.[B]*

The boy lived with his mother in a little house.

7. *Do the Laia Flower figure from "The Park" as found on page 74.[C]*

CRADLE05

His mother wanted to do everything she could to make her boy happy and healthy. She decided to make a big vegetable garden in the back yard to grow fresh fruits and vegetables for her boy. She also grew flowers and this is one of the flowers that she grew.

Then the mother thought he would like a dog. She got him a dog and the boy loved the dog. He taught the dog how to fetch sticks. The dog would run after the stick and bring it back to the boy. The boy would throw the stick and the dog would bring it back.

1. *With your fingers pointing away from you, hang the string on L1 and R1. Grasp the string hanging down with 3, 4, and 5 on both hands.*

2. *(Illus. Dog01) 2 bends down over the string held between L1 and R1.*

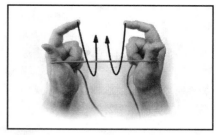

DOG01

3. *(Illus. Dog02) 2 points down and away, picking up the string near the first knuckle as 2 moves back to position. The hands should remain close together.*

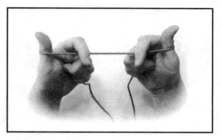

DOG02

4. *(Illus. Dog03) L1 picks up the string going between R1 and R2.*

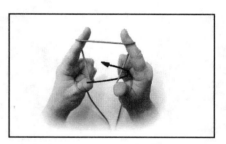

DOG03

5. *(Illus. Dog04) R1 picks up the string going between L1 and L2. An hourglass shape is formed.*

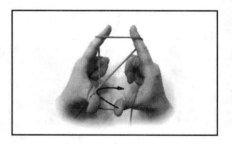

DOG04

6. *(Illus. Dog05) 3, 4, and 5 stop holding their strings. Pull the hands apart.*

DOG05

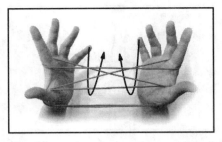

DOG06

7. *(Illus. Dog06) 5 enters the 1 loop from below. 5 pulls back the transverse 1f string as it moves back to position.*

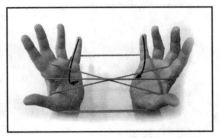

DOG07

8. *(Illus. Dog07) R5 hooks down on L2f and holds it to the palm. L5 hooks down on L1f and holds it to the palm.*

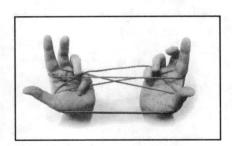

DOG08

9. *(Illus. Dog08) The loops on 5 slip off 5.*

DOG09

10. *(Illus. Dog09) 1 hooks down on the 1f string that goes to the middle of the figure, allowing the other string on the back of 1 to slip over 1. 1 straightens back up, retaining the hooked string.*

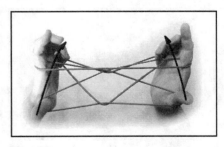

DOG10

11. *(Illus. Dog10) 1 goes into the 2 loop from below.*

12. *(Illus. Dog11) Navajo the strings on 1.*

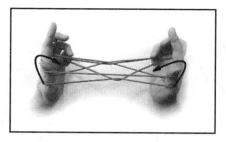

DoG11

13. *(Illus. Dog12) Release 2 loops.*

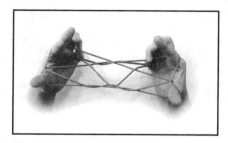

DoG12

14. *(Illus. Dog13) Hold your hands so they are facing you. From behind the figure, R2 enters between the strings labeled a and b.*

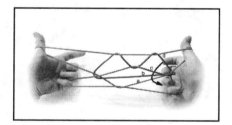

DoG13

15. *(Illus. Dog14) R2 pulls back on b and c. R2 moves on top of d.*

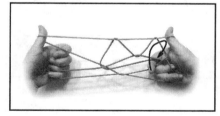

DoG14

16. *(Illus. Dog15) R2 then moves to bottom of figure and hooks up 5f (Illus. Dog16) and pulls it back through the loops already on R2. Those loops slip off R2.*

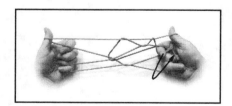

DoG15

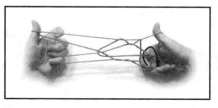

DoG16

DOG17

17. (Illus. Dog17) L5 releases its loop which then hangs down in the middle of the figure.

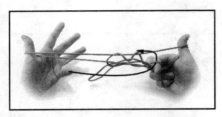

DOG18

18. (Illus. Dog18) L5 enters the R2 loop from the fingertip side and removes the loop. Pull the figure taut.

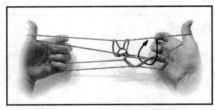

DOG19

19. (Illus. Dog19) There are two strings that go from the R palmar string and wrap around the 5f string. R2 enters the R1 loop from behind, then goes into the R5 loop. R2 lifts up those two strings over the two strings that go to the middle of the figure.

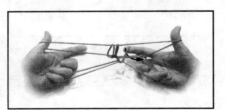

DOG20

20. (Illus. Dog20) As R2 moves behind those strings, a section of the R palmar string appears next to R2. R2 grasps that string.

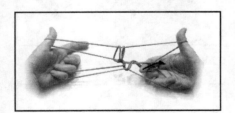

DOG21

21. (Illus. Dog21) At the same time, release R1 and R5. Put R3, R4, and R5 into the loop with R2.

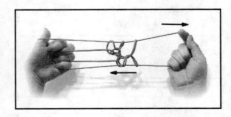

DOG22

22. As you pull your hands apart, the dog will run to the left (Illus. Dog22).[D]

Do the first figure from this story again.

The mother said, "It's almost time for lunch. You don't have to take a nap, just go in and have a rest while I go out in the garden to gather vegetables for our lunch." So the boy went in and lay down in his hammock. He didn't mean to go to sleep but that gently rocking hammock put him right to sleep.

Nobody knew it, but a terrible ogre came by the house. He peeked in the window and saw the boy asleep in the hammock. He said to himself, "The boy will make a perfect lunch for me." And the ogre took the boy to his cave in the mountains.

1. Opening A. (Illus. Salt01) 2, 3, 4, 5 bend down into 1 loop and flips it up over the back of the hands.

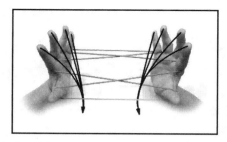

SALT01

2. (Illus. Salt02) 1 goes under the near hand strings but over the far hand string to bring back the 5f string.

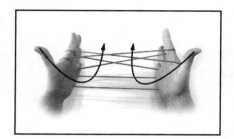

SALT02

3. (Illus. Salt03) 1 picks up 2f.

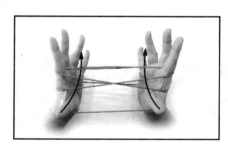

SALT03

4. (Illus. Salt04) 5 releases its loop.

SALT04

5. (Illus. Salt05) 5 picks up 1f.

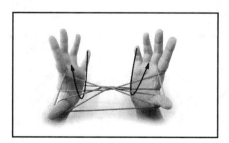

SALT05

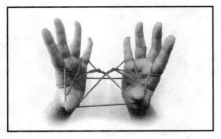

SALT06

6. (Illus. Salt06) Release 1 loops.

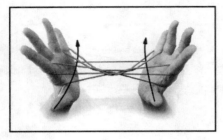

SALT07

7. (Illus. Salt07) 1 picks up 5n.

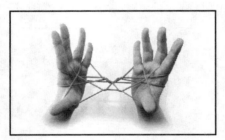

SALT08

8. (Illus. Salt08) R1 and R2 pick up L2n and the near hand string where they pass closest to 2 (Illus. Salt09). Place both strings over L1.

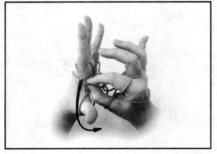

SALT9

9. (Illus. Salt10) Navajo the bottom loop on L1 over those two loops.

SALT10

10. Repeat Steps 8 through 9 on R.

11. *(Illus. Salt11) Tip 2 down into the triangle that forms between 1 and 2 (Illus. Salt12). Release the 5 loops. Point 1 and 2 down and away from you. At the same time flip the hand loop around to the front of the figure. Allow the loop to move above 1.*

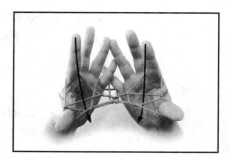

SALT11

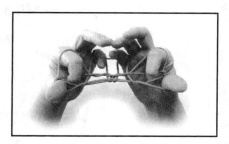

SALT12

The ogre said to the boy, "The first thing I'm going to do is cut off your hand!" The boy was afraid. Let me show you how the ogre meant to do this.

Meanwhile, the mother found out the ogre had taken her boy. She was determined to rescue him but she didn't know where his cave was. She went back out into the garden to ask one of the birds because birds fly high and they see everything.

12. *(Illus. Salt13) 1 hooks down on this string, allowing the loops already on 1 to slide off. Extend. (Illus. salt14)[E]*

Do the Cut Your Hand figure from the section on Sharing String Figures with Children as found on page 19.[F]

Do the Flying Bird figure Steps 1 through 8 from "The Park" as found on page 78 .

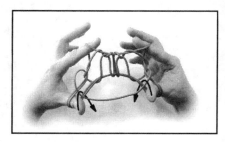

SALT13

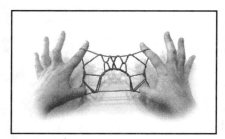

SALT14

Here is the bird. See his wings? He said, "I know where the ogre's cave is. Follow me." So the mother followed the bird to the ogre's cave.

Pull hands apart and loops will move from R to L.

The ogre saw the mother come up the path. He came out of the cave and said, "What are you doing here?"

She said, "I have come to rescue my boy."

"Ha! He will be my lunch. You will be my dinner."

The mother had brought with her a rope that could cut anything.

1. *Hold up string.*

Before the ogre could grab her she threw the rope over his head once and twice

2. *Hang the string around your neck. Pick up the string closest to R and wrap it around your neck again.*

3. *Hold the string hanging in front of you in Position 1. Opening A, making sure to take up the L palmar string first.*

4. *(Illus. Cutneck01) Release 5 loops.*

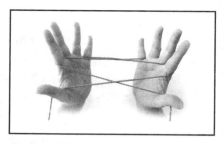

CUTNECK01

5. *(Illus. Cutneck02) 3, 4, and 5 enter the 2 loop from below.*

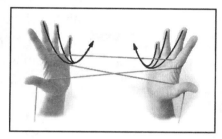

CUTNECK02

6. *(Illus. Cutneck03) Turn both hands so they are facing you. 2, 3, 4, and 5 grab down on the strings crossing in front of them. Turn your hands down and away from you so you are looking at the backs of your hands. Two strings are at the top and one strings hangs below.*

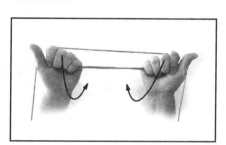

CUTNECK03

and cut off his head.

7. *(Illus. Cutneck04) Put your head into this loop held between the hands. Pull quickly on the single string that was at the bottom of the loop (Illus. Cutneck05) and the loop will come off your neck.*[G]

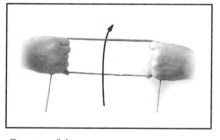

CUTNECK04

Do the first figure in this story again.

Then she took her boy back home where he took a nap in his hammock and they lived happily ever after.

CUTNECK05

Notes:

[A]This is the beginning figure in the game of Cat's Cradle.

[B]Siberian House

[C]Laia Flower

[D]Little Dog With Big Ears was collected by Diamond Jenness (Gryski, *Super String Games* 76).

[E]The Salt Cave figure came from Hawaii (Gryski, *Many Stars* 62). It is a variation of Jacob's Ladder.

[F]Cutting the Hand is an Inuit figure (Gryski, *Cat's Cradle* 28).

[G]Cut Off Your Head is described as Cheating the Hangman by Gryski (*Cat's Cradle* 32). It comes from the Philippines.

18. "Going Fishing" by Brian Cox

Brian Cox is from Winnipeg, Canada. He is well known for his involvement with children, origami, and string figures. He recently retired from his job as counselor at a youth center where he worked with incarcerated youth. He shared his interests with the kids he counseled and felt that mastering origami and string figures gave them confidence.

Brian wrote this story with his daughter almost 20 years ago. They were traveling in an old school bus and performing in Manitoba. Brian says the story was developed with the thought that when you return to school, often you are asked to write about what you did during vacation. Their thought was to tell the story in string.

Sara and I were sitting one day in an Apache teepee.

1. *Hold out L with palm facing up. Hang the string on L so that it lays between L1 and L2 and to the right of L5. (Illus. Teepee01) R grabs the two strings hanging under L. Bring them up over the fingers so that the left string now passes between L2 and L3 and the right string passes between L4 and L5. These two strings are hanging over the L palmar string.*

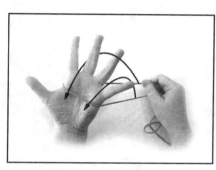

TEEPEE01

2. *(Illus. Teepee02) With R1 and R2, reach under the L palmar string and pull the two strings so that they now go behind the L palmar string.*

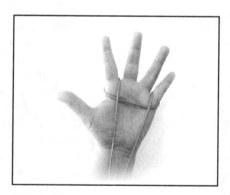

TEEPEE02

3. *(Illus. Teepee03) R comes from underneath into the loop hanging from L so that the loop rests on the R wrist. R1 enters the L2 loop from above and picks up the L2f string closest to the finger before it crosses under the L palmar string. R5 enters the L5 loop from above and picks up the L5n string closest to the finger before it crosses under the L palmar string.*

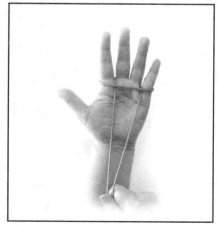

TEEPEE03

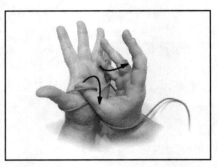

TEEPEE04

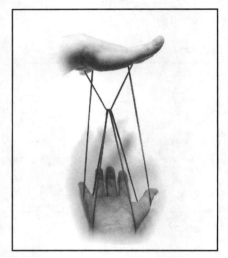

TEEPEE05

4. (Illus. Teepee04) They return to position. Make sure the loop stays on the right wrist. Turn the hands so that R is on the bottom and L is on the top. (Illus. Teepee05)[A]

Do the Apache Door figure from the story, "The Leprechaun," found on page 89.[B]

Point to tight finger loops.

Dissolve the figure, peer through the loop.

Do the Witch's Broom of Fish Spear figure from the Basic String Figures Instructions section as found on page 6.[C]

It was getting a little warm inside, so we went over to the door. Now it only makes sense that if you have an Apache teepee, you'll also have an Apache door.

We undid the catches

and stepped out through the opening.

What a gorgeous day it was! What should we do on such a fine day? Let's go fishing! So Sara went over and got the fish net, and I went over to the rack and picked up a Fish Spear

and off we went down the path to the meadow.

Now in the meadow, there were all sorts of neat things, like furry little animals and bees and flowers. Sara and I sat down to have a bit of a rest and a snack and along came a beautiful butterfly.

1. *(Illus. NButterfly01) Hold the string in both hands so there is a straight segment between the hands.*

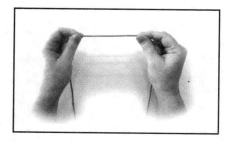

NBUTTERFLY01

2. *(Illus. NButterfly02) Twist this segment so a circle forms.*

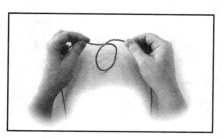

NBUTTERFLY02

3. *(Illus. NButterfly03) From behind, insert 2 into the circle.*

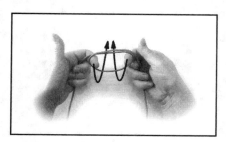

NBUTTERFLY03

4. *(Illus. NButterfly04) Continue holding the string with 3, 4, and 5. 2 twists down and back up so that an X forms between the hands.*

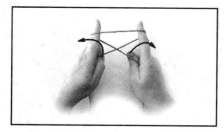

NBUTTERFLY04

5. *(Illus. NButterfly05) 1 picks up the bottom strings of the X from behind. 3, 4, and 5 release the strings they were holding. Extend.*

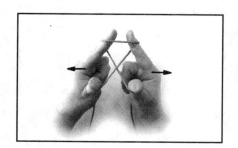

NBUTTERFLY05

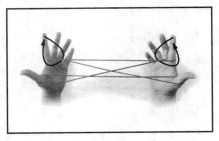

NBUTTERFLY06

6. *(Illus. NButterfly06) Rotate 2 away from you and back up 5 times.*

NBUTTERFLY07

7. *(Illus. NButterfly07) 1 shares the 2 loop, keeping the two strings on 1 apart.*

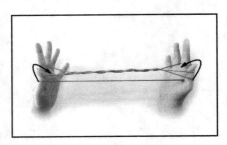

NBUTTERFLY08

8. *(Illus. NButterfly08) Navajo the 1 loops.*

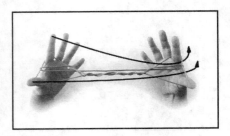

NBUTTERFLY09

9. *(Illus. NButterfly09) Hang the R2 loop on L2 and the R1 loop on L1 (Illus. NButterfly10).*

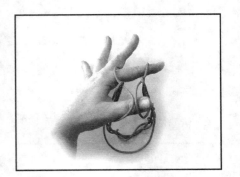

NBUTTERFLY10

10. *(Illus. NButterfly11) R3, R4, and R5 removes the first L1 loop from the fingertip side. R1 removes the remaining L1 loop from underneath.*

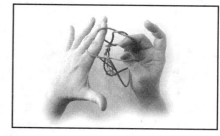

NButterfly11

This butterfly floated right past us, then went way up into a tree and just sort of sat there. Sara said to me, "Dad, go up the tree and try to catch that butterfly." So I tied my shoes really tight (you don't want to climb a tree with untied shoe laces), and started to climb the tree.

11. *(Illus. NButterfly12) L3, L4, and L5 remove the L2 loop from the fingertip side. L1 removes the L2 loop from underneath. Extend. A coil will appear in the middle of the figure. 3, 4, and 5 grab down the near string of their loop and the 1f string. 2 enters the 3, 4, 5 loop from behind and pulls up to tighten and extend the figure. The loose string that wraps around the figure should go to the left of the coiled "proboscis" (Illus. nbutterfly13). Move 1 and 2 together and apart to move the butterfly wings.[D]*

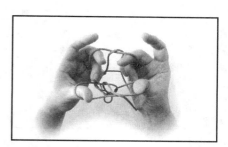

NButterfly12

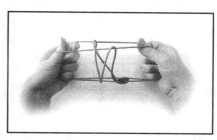

NButterfly13

1. *Opening A (Illus. Climb01) 5 goes over all strings and picks up 1n.*

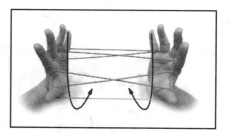

Climb01

2. *(Illus. Climb02) Navajo the loops on 5. Make sure the string that comes over 5 stays beyond the 2 loop.*

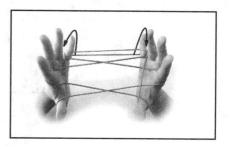

Climb02

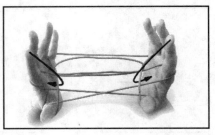

CLIMB03

3. *(Illus. Climb03) 2 hooks down over the palmar string passing in front of it.*

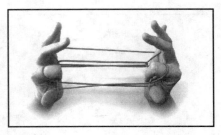

CLIMB04

4. *(Illus. Climb04) Release all loops except where 2 is holding down the string. Grasp 2 loop with all fingers.*

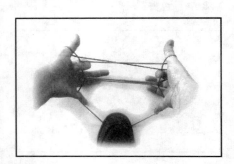

CLIMB05

5. *(Illus. Climb05) Hold the figure close to the floor. Step onto 5f with your foot.*

I climbed way up to where the branches begin

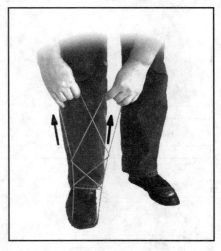

CLIMB06

6. *(Illus. Climb06) As you straighten up, alternate pulling your hands straight up and the figure climbs up.[E]*

and disappeared inside the branches. I was just about to catch the butterfly when along came a big black fly.

1. *Put string around 1 and extend hands until taut. (String shown is shorter than normal.)*

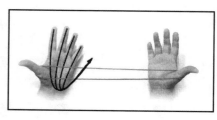

MOSQUITO01

2. *(Illus. Mosquito01) Keeping the string taut, move L2, L3, L4, and L5 under the strings so that the string lies on the back of L.*

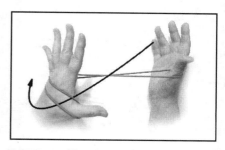

MOSQUITO02

3. *(Illus. Mosquito02) R5 picks up the two strings passing behind L1 and L2 and returns to position. Then push strings as far down on the fingers as possible.*

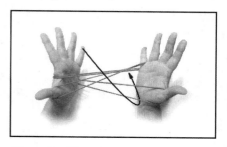

MOSQUITO03

4. *(Illus. Mosquito03) (Normal string is shown.) L5 picks up the two strings on R1 and returns to position.*

You know what flies are like, always bugging you. The next thing I knew, the butterfly had flown away, so I caught the fly instead! Now if you happen to catch a fly in your hands, they'll walk around inside and when their feet tickle your palms you'll want to take a peek. But flies are pretty fast, and if you don't peek fast enough the fly will get away.

5. *(Illus. Mosquito04) Keeping all strings in place, R1 and R2 picks up the two strings on the back of L.*

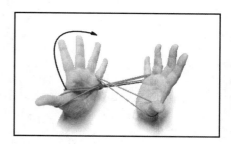

MOSQUITO04

6. *(Illus. Mosquito05) Pass them over the four fingers on L, pulling as far to the right as possible and letting go of the two strings only. Make all remaining strings taut.*

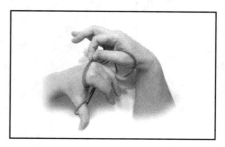

MOSQUITO05

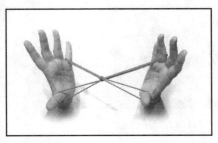

MOSQUITO06

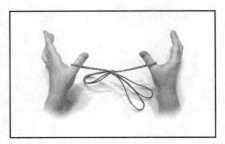

MOSQUITO07

7. *The fly should appear midway between the two hands (Illus. Mosquito06).*

8. *Clap your hands together. While your hands are closed, palms together, release the strings on 5 while keeping the strings around 1.*

9. *(Illus. Mosquito07) Pull out and the fly will have disappeared.*[F]

So I climbed back down the tree and told Sara about the butterfly and she said, "That's OK, Dad, at least you tried. Let's get going, we're still going fishing and we're already late."

We decided to cut through the forest. Now when you go through the forest it's best to let the forest know you are there, but don't make too much noise or you'll scare all the creatures away. We walked along the path, and over in the corner we spotted a shy little rabbit.

This rabbit was so shy all you could see was his ears and his head sticking above a log. We watched the rabbit for a while, tip toed around him so as not to disturb him, got back on the path, started toward the lake, and there sitting right in the middle of the lake was a duck with big feet.

Do the Rabbit figure from "The Park" as found on page 81.[G]

1. *Opening A (Illus. Crow01). 2, 3, 4, and 5 tip down into the 1 loop from above. Flip the 1 loop over the backs of the hands. Be sure that 1 is not inside the loop that is now going around the backs of the hands.*

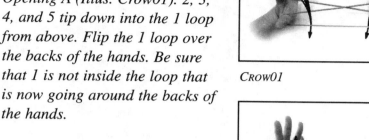

CROW01

2. *(Illus. Crow02) 1 removes the 2 loops from below.*

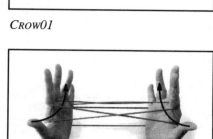

CROW02

3. *(Illus. Crow03) R picks up the string on the back of L and places it onto L3.*

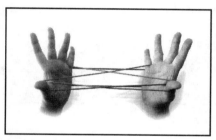

CROW03

4. *(Illus. Crow04) L picks up the string on the back of R and places it onto R3.*

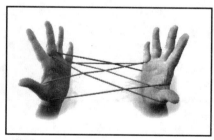

CROW04

5. *(Illus. Crow05) 5 goes over 3f and picks up its own 5n string.*

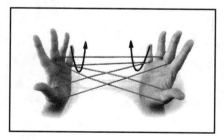

CROW05

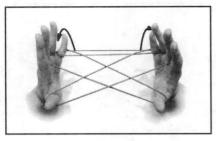

CROW06

6. *(Illus. Crow06) Navajo the strings on 5.*

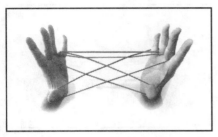

CROW07

7. *(Illus. Crow07) Release 1 and extend (Illus. Crow08). Take the double string in the middle of the figure in your mouth. Bring your hands below your mouth to display the feet.[H]*

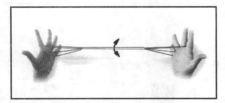

CROW08

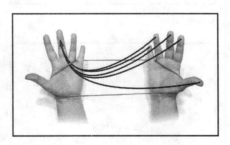

FISH01

1. *Position 1 (Illus. Fish01). Put all of R under the L palmar string so the string hangs down on the R wrist.*

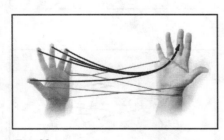

FISH02

2. *(Illus. Fish02) Put all of L under the R palmar string so the string hangs down on the L wrist.*

We watched the duck for a while, then headed to the other side of the lake where our favorite spot is. We started checking our gear, making sure the spear was sharp and the net wasn't torn, because you really can't catch fish if you have holes in your net! Everything looked pretty good. We approached the edge of the lake, and just there waiting for us were two of the biggest fish

3. *(Illus. Fish03) 2 goes into the 5 loop from above and pulls back on the 5n string. 2 pulls the 5n string over the top of the 1f string (Illus. Fish04). Pull up on that 1f string so that the first string falls off. 1 releases its loop.*

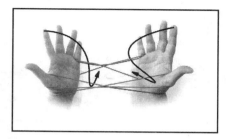

Fish03

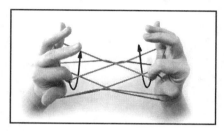

Fish04

4. *(Illus. Fish05) Transfer 2 loop to 1.*

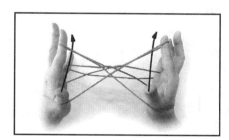

Fish05

5. *(Illus. Fish06) Take loop off the back of L and put in Position 1 over L1 and L5. Take loop off the back of R and put in Position 1 over R1 and R5.*

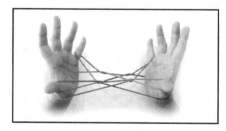

Fish06

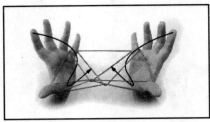

FISH07

6. *(Illus. Fish07) As before, 2 goes into the 5 loop from above and pulls back on 5n. 2 pulls the 5n string over the top of 1f (Illus. Fish08). Pull up on 1f to make a loop on 2.*

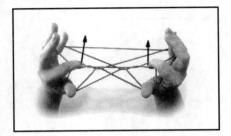

FISH08

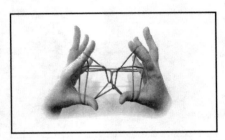

FISH09

7. *(Illus. Fish09) Remove 1 from loops and do not extend.*

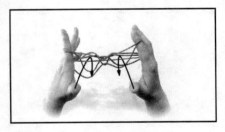

FISH10

8. *(Illus. Fish10) 1 re-enters those loops from the front side, reaches through and brings back the 5f string. The other loops on 1 slip off.*

Sara and I had ever seen! We got the net ready and were just about ready to throw it when the fish swam away.

Just when we thought all our fun was over, Sarah reminded me that we brought some string with us. This reminded us of a story we learned from a little girl called Fisherman's Nightmare. Now what she did was she wrapped it around her fingers like this,

around her thumb like this,

9. *(Illus. fish11) Release 5 and extend until the fish appear. You may need to arrange them (Illus. fish12).*

10. *Pull hands apart until fish disappear.[1]*

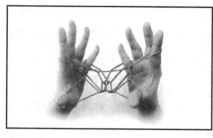

FISH11

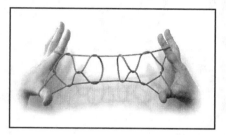

FISH12

1. *Hold L flat with palm up, fingers pointing away from you. Hang the string on the palm so that it hangs between L1 and L2 and to the right of L5 (Illus. Fisher01). R grabs the strings hanging under L and pulls them up over the fingers of L so that the left string passes between L2 and L3 and the right string between L4 and L5.*

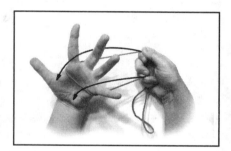

FISHER01

2. *(Illus. Fisher02) R is still grasping those strings. Twist R away from you to the left so that the string coming from L4 and L5 is on the bottom and the string coming from L2 and L3 is on the top. Keeping those strings in that same position, lay them over the back of L1.*

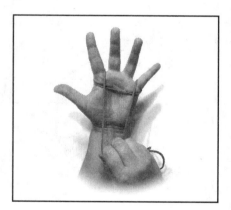

FISHER02

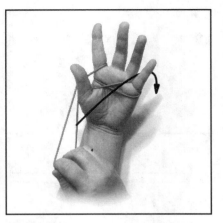

3. *(Illus. Fisher03) Bring the bottom string from L1 and put it between L4 and L5. Let it hang behind L.*

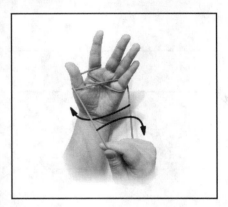

4. *(Illus. Fisher04) R takes the loop of string that is hanging from L1 and L5 and twists it over to the right so that an X forms.*

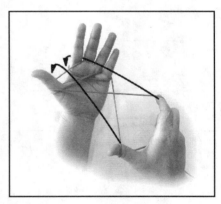

5. *(Illus. Fisher05) Pull it over L2 so that L2 goes into the top part of the X. Tug on the strings as they hang behind the hand.*

and gave it a good tug to make it secure

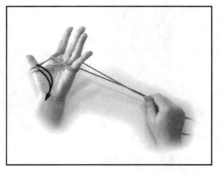

6. *(Illus. Fisher06) Let loop hang behind hand. R then removes the 2 loops from L1 and pulls them out as far as they will go.*

then she blew on it, and it came off just like that.

7. *(Illus. Fisher07) Pull these strings back over the fingers of L. The two left strings go between L2 and L3 and the two right strings will go between L4 and L5 (Illus. Fisher08).*

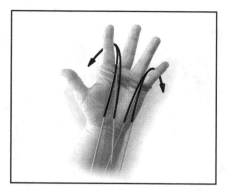

FISHER07

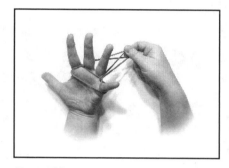

FISHER08

Wow! We were starting to get really excited and began to play some more.

We found out that string has all sorts of uses: you can use it as a back scratcher.

9. *(Illus. Fisher09) Pull up on the straight palmar string and the strings will come right off the hand.[J]*

FISHER09

It can also teach you how to dance, sort of like drying your bum with a towel.

1. *Holding the string between your hands, raise L and move the string over your head so that it is now on your back. R will be near your waist. Scratch your back by moving the string back and forth (Illus. Towel01).*

2. *Move L down to your waist. Put the string behind you and pretend you're drying your bottom.*

TOWEL101

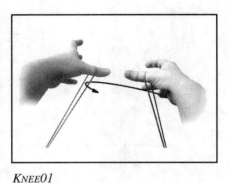

KNEE01

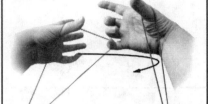

KNEE02

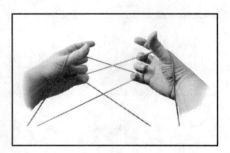

KNEE03

STAR01

3. *Hold the string behind your knees between both hands. Bring it to the front. Hold the loop on R1 and L1. (Illus. Knee01) R5 grabs L1n.*

2. *(Illus. Knee02) L5 goes through the L1 loop and grabs R1f. The hands pull apart as far as they can go (Illus. Knee03).*

3. *As you blow, release the string from L5 and R1. At the same time R and L pull out to the side quickly with the string still on L1 and R5. The string appears to pass through the knees.[K]*

1. *Hang the string on your neck. Twist it twice under your chin. (Illus. Star01) Pull it down into a triangle. L5 and R5 come from underneath to hold the base of the triangle.*

But how do you stop once you've started? You could just take your thumbs out, but that's too easy. You need more of a challenge. Try wrapping the string around your knees,

then blow on it with magic breath. Remember, magic breath is different than bad breath— bad breath will melt the string! So you blow on it with magic breath and step free.

Sara and I were having so much fun, we forgot how late it was getting. The reason we knew it was getting late is because the stars began to come out.

2. *(Illus. Star02) Making sure the string stays hooked on L5 and R5, grasp a portion of the string passing between L5 and R5 with L1 and L2 and R1 and R2.*

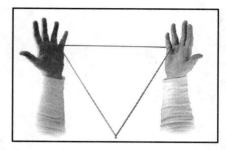

STAR02

3. *(Illus. Star03) Twist it into a loop.*

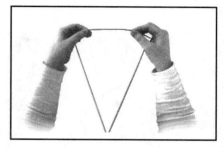

STAR03

4. *(Illus. Star04) Flip the loop away from you and up.*

STAR04

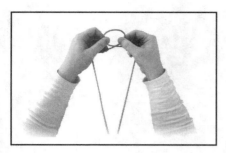

STAR05

5. *(Illus. Star05) L1 and R1 enter the loop. Return to position and extend the fingers. A star will form (Illus. Star06).[L]*

Do The Little Dog With Big Ears figure Steps 1 through 21 from "The Mother and the Ogre" as found on page 95.[M]

STAR06

As you pull your hands apart, the dog will run to the left.

Hold string on 1.

String makes smile (Illus. Smile01).

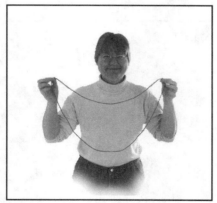

SMILE01

It was time to start heading home. We got back on the path, and as we started getting close to home we heard a familiar sound. What we heard was our pet dog Molly

coming down the path. If you watch real close, you can actually see Molly coming down the path to meet us.

That made us feel kind of neat, which made us think of all the other neat things we did all day like going fishing, chasing butterflies and rabbits, and playing with string. And we learned that string has its own magic. Probably the best magic you can do with string is to take it like this,

stretch it out full, let it sag in the center, and then you can smile at your friends and yourself at the same time.

Thank you very much, that's our string story.

Notes: Brian Cox has accomplished much over the years. He was coordinator of the family area at the Winnipeg Folk Festival for 20 years. He was also the original site coordinator of the Winnipeg International Children's Fest, a four-day event that attracts 35,000 children. He currently is in charge of the Origami venue where annually they assemble a 1,000 paper crane mobile. He has also been involved with The Teddy Bear Picnic where children bring their teddy bears to a local hospital to be fixed. The event provides children with an opportunity to learn about going to the hospital and raises money for the children's hospital's research foundation. Brian has also been a performer on a children's TV program and produced a cable TV series on origami.

[A]Jayne learned Apache Teepee from an Apache woman from New Mexico at the St. Louis Expedition (246).

[B]Apache Door is the first figure in Jayne's book. It was collected from an Apache girl from New Mexico (12). Abraham gives Mexican Hurdle as another name (68).

[C]Abraham indicates that the Fish Spear is one of the most widely distributed figures (17). Other names given are A Brush House, Pitching a Tent, and A Balance (20). Gryski adds Duck Spear, Coconut Palm Tree, and Witch's Broom (*Cat's Cradle* 22).

[D]Butterfly was collected by Jayne from two Navajo girls at the St. Louis Worlds Exposition (219).

[E]Man Climbing a Tree is originally from Australia (Gryski, *Cat's Cradle* 44).

[F]Dickey called this figure Knot Slip Trick and said that it strongly resembled Locust of Central Africa, Fly of British Guiana and Fly of New Caledonia (153). He suggested it could be called Mosquito. Pellowski uses this figure for her Mosquito string story (5).

[G]Rabbit is a Klamath Indian figure (Jayne 79).

[H]Duck With Big Feet is the name that Brian Cox gives this figure. This figure was discussed in the Mouse Face story. The method used here to make it is the more traditional one. The end result is the same.

[I]Jayne called this figure No Name (176).

[J]Brian originally knew this figure without a name. Later a man who was a navy sailor said he knew it as Fisherman's Nightmare from Italy. Abraham calls it The Disappearing Loops. He had heard it called The Smith's Secret (33).

[K]The author has not located this figure in any other publication.

[L]This appears to be an original figure of Cox's.

[M]The Little Dog with Big Ears was collected by Diamond Jenness (Gryski, *Super* 76).

19. "Jack and the Beanstalk: David Novak's Rhyme and String Version" by David Novak

David Novak is a professional storyteller. He has been Master Storyteller for the Disney Institute at Walt Disney World in Florida. You can see his performance of Jack and the Beanstalk on the *Tell Me a Story* videotape.

You need to use a string longer than usual for this story.

This story uses the Jacob's Ladder figure frequently. The directions for it are found in Chapter I on page 9.

Do the figure from the story "Totanguak," found on page 46, Steps 1 through 5.

This is the story of a boy named Jack

Who lived with his mother in a run-down shack.

Jack and his mother were as poor as the dirt

And that's a situation that really hurt.

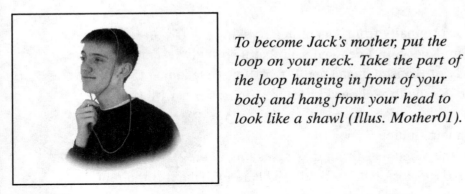

To become Jack's mother, put the loop on your neck. Take the part of the loop hanging in front of your body and hang from your head to look like a shawl (Illus. Mother01).

MOTHER01

His mother said,
"Jack, we'll manage
somehow,

Go out to the market
and sell the cow.

Tie a tether 'round
Milky White

Go out in the
morning and come
back at night."

So Jack jumped up
in the morning light

And he tied a tether
'round Milky White

Then Jack headed
out with his cow on
a tether

When a strange
little man hopped
out of the heather.

He said, "Son,
you're a climber,
now I can tell

That you'll go far
and you'll do well.

You got your sights
on the heights

You got your eye on
the sky,

You're a capable,
intelligent kind of
guy.

But to get you
started, the thing
you need

Is a little bit of help
in the form of a
seed.

Form Jacob's Ladder.

*(Illus. Tether00) With your teeth, bite
the center X in Jacob's Ladder and
pull.*

*Release loops on 2 and pull figure
tight.*

*Slide the string from your mouth up
beneath your nose. This is the tether
on Milky White (Illus. Tether01).*

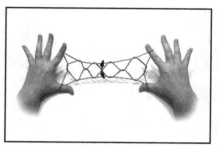

TETHER00

TETHER01

Take the cow figure and grasp both ends in one hand. Hold the other hand under the figure to show the pouch (Illus. Pouch01).

Now in my pouch I have some beans of power,

You plant these beans you'll get more than a flower,

You'll get a beanstalk as tall as a star

Why these magic beans will take you far.

So I'll take your cow for the beans, now that's an even trade

And that's the way a stock-market is made."

So Jack made the trade and got home that night,

But it gave his mother a terrible fright.

She saw what he'd done, sat down and wept.

But Jack planted those beans before he slept.

Early next morning to his surprise, There was a beanstalk of enormous size.

So he hopped out of bed and he started to climb,

Reached the top and had a wonderful time

Until he heard some thunder that made him afeard.

For in stomped a giant with a big stringy beard

Form Jacob's Ladder and hold vertically. Lower the figure to show Jack climbing up (Illus. Beanstalk01).

BEANSTALK01

Continue with the Jacob's Ladder figure (Illus. Beard00). Bite the lower string and pull down.

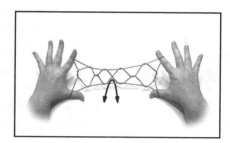

BEARD00

Saying, "Fee, Fie, Fo, Fum!

I smell the blood of an Englishman.

Be he live or be he dead

I'll grind his bones to make my bread."

But the giant's wife said, "Fee, Fie, Fo, my foot!

Release strings on 1 and place 2 loops around ears. This is the giant's beard (Illus. Beard01).

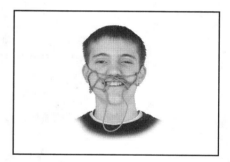

BEARD01

Flip the beard up on top of your head (Illus. Wife01).

WIFE01

Now you sit down and you stay put.
I've worked all morning to make this feast,
So you'll eat it, and like it at the very least.
You sit down and you keep quiet.
Besides, little boys are too rich for your diet.
They're all made of sodium, sugar, and lard.
And you ever try to cook one? It's much too hard.
You can't even get them to wash their face,
Without them getting mud all over the place!"
So the giant ate his meal, then he started to snore
As Jack crept out of the kitchen door.
But before he left, Jack made so bold
As to take that giant's bag of gold.

Take the figure off your ears and hold the two ends in one hand. It will look similar to the pouch.

That bag of gold sure made his mother smile.
Then they were happy for quite awhile.
But another time Jack went up that stalk
And he hid as he heard the giant talk,

Form the giant's beard again.

Saying "Fee, Fie, Fo, Fum!
I smell the blood of an Englishman.
Be he live or be he dead,
I'll grind his bones to make my bread."
But the giant's wife said, "There aren't any little boys about!

Put the giant's beard up on your head again.

Now you eat what I made, or you eat out!"
So he ate his meal, then he snored once more,
As Jack tippy-toed across the floor.
This time Jack took the Magic Hen.
Then he climbed back down that stalk again.

Jacob's Ladder held vertically. Move up to show Jack climbing down.

Now when they tell that hen to lay,

They get gold eggs in the nest each day.

1. *Begin with Jacob's Ladder. (Illus. Eggs01) Move hands together. L5 removes the loop from R2. R5 removes the R1 loop.*

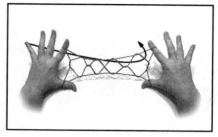

EGGS01

3. *(Illus. Eggs02) R1 removes the loop from L1.*

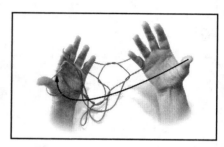

EGGS02

4. *(Illus. Eggs03) L1 takes the loop from L2, untwisting it during the transfer.*

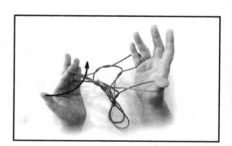

EGGS03

But Jack wasn't done. No, not yet.

There was one thing more that he wanted to get.

So he climbed back up that stalk once more,

And he hid as he heard that giant roar

5. *(Illus. Eggs04) Slowly pull the hands apart and the eggs will appear in the center of the figure (Illus. Eggs05).*

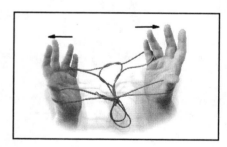

EGGS04

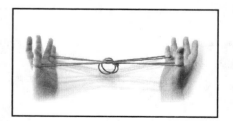

EGGS05

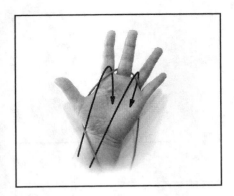

HARPAXE01

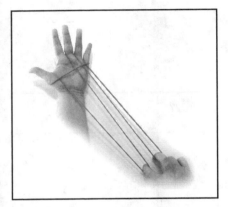

HARPAXE02

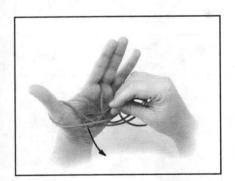

HARPAXE03

Form the giant's beard again.

1. *(Illus. HarpAxe01) Place the string on the left hand, hanging it on 1, 3, and 5. Reach under the string hanging down. R1 and R2 pull down on the strings that pass in front of L2 and L4.*

2. *Continue pulling downward so that the long loop comes up and crosses on front of the strings you are pulling. This is the harp (Illus. HarpAxe02).*

3. *Move R1 and R2 from side to side to make it sing (Illus. HarpAxe02).*

4. *Continuing from the harp figure, R1 and R2 pinch their loops together. They bring them down through the hole that is formed by the loop on L3 and the L palmar string.*

5. *(Illus. HarpAxe03) Pull the loops through, making sure they aren't twisted.*

"Fee, Fie, Fo, Fum!

I smell the blood of an Englishman.

Be he live or be he dead,

I'll grind his bones to make my bread.

Now woman, don't tell me that he's not here.

I smell little boy, it's strong and clear!

I'll skin him alive, I'll tan his hide,

I'll dip him in batter and I'll have him fried!"

But Jack stayed hid, that kid was smart.

After awhile the giant lost heart,

Ate his meal and once more slept,

As out of hiding Jack carefully crept

To the cupboard in the castle with the harp that sings,

But the harp cried out from its golden strings

singing, "Help! Help! Help!"

That woke up the giant, who went for Jack.

But lickety-split, the kid climbed back,

6. *(Illus. HarpAxe04) Release L3.*

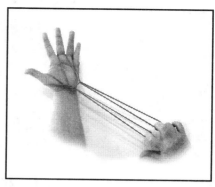

HARPAXE04

Grabbed his axe, chopped and chopped,

Until that ugly ol' giant dropped.

7. *(Illus. HarpAxe05) Hold the figure horizontally. Make chopping motions by moving L up and down.*

8. *Hold the axe figure vertically, L on top. Release L5 and the loop on R2. Quickly pull the hands apart and the figure dissolves.*

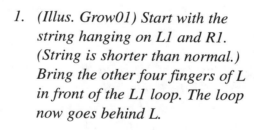

HARPAXE05

So Jack survived and his mother too.

But after that, what did they do?

Well, Jack became famous in his home town,

For spreading his new-made wealth around.

For it's just as true now, as it was long ago.

You've got to spread the wealth, for good things to grow.

1. *(Illus. Grow01) Start with the string hanging on L1 and R1. (String is shorter than normal.) Bring the other four fingers of L in front of the L1 loop. The loop now goes behind L.*

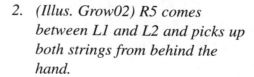

GROW01

2. *(Illus. Grow02) R5 comes between L1 and L2 and picks up both strings from behind the hand.*

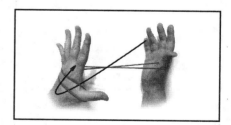

GROW02

3. *(Illus. Grow03) (Normal string is shown.) L5 comes over all the strings and picks up the two strings on R1.*

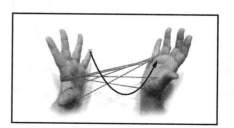

GROW03

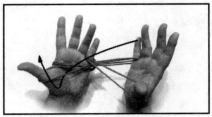

GROW04

4. (Illus. Grow04) L5 returns to position but the hands should stay close together. Transfer the loop on L1 to R5.

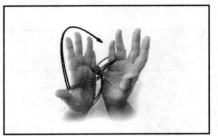

GROW05

5. (Illus. Grow05) R1 and R2 take the strings from the back of L and moves them over L2, L3, L4, and L5 into the middle of the figure.

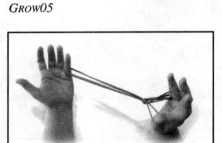

GROW06

6. (Illus. Grow06) Extend and pull on the strings on L5 to tighten the knot.

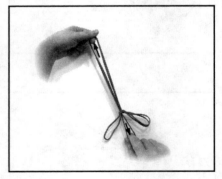

GROW07

7. (Illus. Grow07) Hold the figure vertically. Release the loops on R5. Pull on R1 and the loops will rise to the top (Illus. Grow08). (When using an even longer string the loops will have further to rise.)

Notes: This story uses the traditional Jacob's Ladder and Siberian House figures but the rest are David Novak's original figures. Tina Eaves originally recorded the directions for these figures in the Winter/Spring, 1994 issue of *Storytelling World*.

GROW08

The List of Figures

Illustrations used in each chapter in order

Chapter I: Overview and Instructions

2. Basic String Figure Instructions

5. Using String Figures With Children

Chapter II: The Stories

1. "The Balloon"

String Stories: A Creative, Hands-On Approach for Engaging Children in Literature

About String Figures. 26 June 1999. International String Figure Association. 27 Mar. 2002 <http://www.isfa.org/isfa1.htm>.

Abraham, A. Johnston. *String Figures.* Algonac, MI: Reference Publications, Inc., 1988.

"A Story About String: String Stories from New Mexico's Storyfiesta™." Rio Rancho, NM: Storytellers International™, n.d.

Baadh, Valerie. *Healthy Play for Children.* 8 Oct. 2001. Mrs. Baadh's Playstrings. 27 Mar. 2002 <http://www.playstrings.com/index.htm>.

Baadh, Valerie. *How To Make Your Hands Dance.* 8 Oct. 2001. Mrs. Baadh's Playstrings. 27 Mar. 2002 <http://www.playstrings.com/dancing.htm>.

Ball, W. W. Rouse. *Fun With String Figures.* New York: Dover, 1971.

D'Antoni, Joseph. "Plinthios Brokhos: The Earliest Account of a String Figure Construction." *Bulletin of the International String Figure Association* 4 (1997): 90-94.

Darsie, Richard. *World-Wide Webs: String Figures From Around the World.* 27 Mar. 2002 <http://www.darsie.net/string/>.

DeWitt, Sorena. *String Figures From Around the World.* Torrance, CA: Heian International, 1995.

DeWitt, Sorena. *String Figures From Around the World II.* Torrance, CA: Heian International, 1995.

Dickey, Lyle Alexander. *String Figures from Hawaii, Including Some From New Hebrides and Gilbert Islands.* Honolulu: Bernice P. Bishop Museum, 1928.

Fascinating String Figures. Mineola, NY: Dover, 1999.

Field, Edward. *Eskimo Song and Stories.* New York: Delacore Press, 1973.

Gryski, Camilla. *Cat's Cradle, Owl's Eyes: A Book of String Games.* New York: William Morrow, 1984.

Gryski, Camilla. *Many Stars & More String Games.* New York: William Morrow, 1985.

Gryski, Camilla. *Super String Games.* New York: Morrow Junior Books, 1987.

Haddon, Kathleen. *String Games for Beginners.* Cambridge: W Heffer & Sons, 1974.

Helfman, Elizabeth, and Harry Helfman. *Strings On Your Fingers: How to Make String Figures.* New York: William Morrow, 1965.

International String Figure Association. 23 Mar. 2002. 27 Mar. 2002
    <http://www.isfa.org>.

Jayne, Caroline Furness. *String Figures and How to Make Them.* New York: Dover,
    1962.

Johnson, Anne Akers. *Cat's Cradle: A Book of String Figures.* Palo Alto, CA: Klutz,
    1993.

Johnson, Anne Akers. *String Games.* Palo Alto, CA: Klutz, 1995.

Kalter, Joanmarie. *The World's Best String Games.* New York: Sterling, 1989.

Leeming, Joseph. *Fun With String.* New York: Dover, 1974.

Maude, Honor. *String Figures From New Caledonia and the Loyalty Islands.*
    Canberra: Home P, 1984.

Meredith, Michael D. "Caroline Furness Jayne (1873-1909)." *Bulletin of the
    International String Figure Association* 4 (1997): 1-7.

Pellowski, Anne. *The Story Vine.* New York: Collier Books, 1984.

Sherman, Mark, and Will Wirt. "String Games of the Navajo." *Bulletin of the
    International String Figure Association* 7 (2000): 119-214.

Stevenson, Gelvin. "What Learning Hands Teach: An Exploration of the
    Psychological, Emotional, and Conceptual Impact of Making String Figures."
    Bulletin of the International String Figure Association 2 (1995): 6-19.

String Magic From Around the World. Perf. David Titus. Videocassette. WRDSMTH
    Productions, 1997.

String Things: Stories, Games and Fun! Perf. Barbara G. Schutzgruber.
    Videocassette. BGSG Storytelling, 1995.

Tell Me a Story Vol. 1. Videocassette. Hometown Entertainment, 1995.

Index

String Stories: A Creative, Hands-On Approach for Engaging Children in Literature

About the Author

Belinda Holbrook is an elementary media specialist for the Davenport Community Schools in Davenport, Iowa. She has a B.A. in Elementary Education from Luther College, Decorah, Iowa, and an M.A. in Library Science from the University of Iowa, Iowa City. She is active in Habitat for Humanity in her community. Hobbies include reading, quilting, and crafts. She and her husband, also a media specialist, have two sons.